BEATRICE SONDERS

HIDING IN PLAIN SIGHT

My Holocaust Story of Survival

A MEMOIR

In loving memory of my parents
Beryl and Reizel Gadziuk,
my younger brother Shalom,
and all of my aunts, uncles, and cousins
who perished at the hands of the Nazis
and those who assisted them.

This book is dedicated to
my three daughters,
my ten grandchildren,
and my seventeen great-grandchildren
…and their children's children.

Foreword by David Salama

As I begin to put the finishing touches on my grandmother's memoir, we are preparing for Passover in the year 2018. Soon, we will sit with our family and retell the story of the Exodus from Egypt. It will be my son Oliver's first Seder. Even though he will not remember this one, he will hopefully sit through many more over the years to come, becoming more and more acquainted with the story of his people and how we were once slaves in Egypt. In fact, probably the most important line of the Passover Haggadah, in my opinion, is the following sentence:

בְּכָל דּוֹר וָדוֹר חַיָּב אָדָם לִרְאוֹת אֶת עַצְמוֹ
כְּאִילוּ הוּא יָצָא מִמִּצְרָיִם.

*"Bchol dor va'dor, chayav adam lir'ot et atsmo K'iloo hu Yatsa
Mee-Mitrayim"*

"In every generation, each person is obligated to view for
themselves as if they had been there and left Egypt."

In other words, we are required to put ourselves in the Exodus narrative and try to imagine that we, as individuals, were witnesses to the slavery of our people and their eventual deliverance out of Egypt to the promised land of Israel. The following memoir entailed a long, complex process, but I like to think that the words in this memoir of the matriarch of my family serve as our own sort of Haggadah. While it's a telling of a story not two-thousand years old, but a mere seventy-five years old, because of my grandmother's survival, we are here today. Because of her, we are a family bound by our connection to this remarkable story of hope, luck, and faith.

It was only in the early 1990s that my grandmother, Bea, began to tell her story, as she kept quiet about much of her experience in the immediate time period after the war. Her children knew bits and pieces of her narrative, but it was never documented in any attempt at preservation for future generations. In beginning to compile this memoir, I transcribed two interviews Bea gave from VHS tapes—one to the Holocaust Museum of South Florida in 1992, and another to the Steven Spielberg Shoah foundation in 1996. A further interview Bea gave on August 27, 2015 to the Holocaust Memorial Center Zekelman Family Campus in Farmington Hills, Michigan was cross-referenced.

Meanwhile, my grandmother's companion, Mort Horowitz, began interviewing her, writing out her story on loose-leaf paper, and turning her memories into a proper narrative. He handed me his copious notes, which I typed up. I then interviewed my grandmother for ten hours over a series of days in 2016 and transcribed those interviews. When I began the process of combining Grandma's interviews, both with me and on video, into one narrative, I enlisted the help of Elizabeth Badovinac, for whom I am so grateful. I would also like to thank Zieva Konvisser and Sarah Dinetz for providing additional editorial suggestions. I would like to also express my appreciation for the help of Alexander Jishkariani who created the graphic images including the maps and family trees, Diren Yardimli for the cover art design and Clark Kenyon for the internal layout and publishing assistance of this memoir.

To find more answers, I contacted the International Tracing Service and found documents of my grandmother's time in the displaced persons (DP) camps in Germany after the war. I also came across her listing on the ship manifest when she and her family came to America in 1949 and dug into the family tree, coming across cousins from both Bea's maternal and paternal lineage. Perhaps most interestingly, I discovered that my grandmother's first cousin, Ida Rosenblum, who is only six months younger than she is, lives in the building next door to her. Due to a family misunderstanding, they did not know each other, despite raising their families less than a mile from one another. I think, therefore, that it is important to recognize the deep wounds the Holocaust created and that, even seventy-five years later, some of these small fragments of shattered families are only now being pieced back together.

In August of 2016, I had the opportunity to travel with my wife to David-Horodok, which is in present-day Belarus, with the David-Horodok organization of Detroit. Together, with other David-Horodok descendants from Detroit and Israel, we walked the cobblestone streets of the town that was once a thriving Jewish community. I found the street on which my grandmother's house once stood. We walked the seven kilometers to the mass grave where Bea's brother and father most likely remain, and later journeyed to Sarny, which is today across the border in the Ukraine. Grandma and her mother walked this 100-kilometer journey together in August of 1941.

There, on the outskirts of town, are three large mounds of earth—the three mass graves in which nearly 18,000 Jews were murdered during the liquidation of the Sarny ghetto. This is the resting place of Bea's mother. Seeing these locations firsthand was a moving and emotional experience and motivated me further to help complete my grandmother's memoir.

I have read and reread Grandma's story. I have walked the streets and towns that she did as a young teenager. I have heard her, with anguish and tears, speak of how her family was murdered. Each time, I've been left amazed by her ability to find hope and maintain faith, even in the most unimaginable horrors. It is my hope that, through this book, the memories of Bea's family will never be forgotten. It is also my hope that future generations of Basia Gadziuk's family take the time to read this family "Haggadah" to understand and appreciate what Bea endured—and ultimately survived.

David Salama
April 2018

Introduction

If Hitler would have had his way, the family I have today—my three daughters, my ten grandchildren, and my seventeen great-grandchildren—wouldn't exist. I would have died in the Holocaust with millions of other Jews, possibly nameless and forgotten among the awful horrors of war and mass genocide. I might have been one of those six million faceless victims the Jews light candles for in memory of, or in one of those mass graves people are still digging up across Europe.

Perhaps I would have been one of the more than four thousand Jews killed in my hometown of David-Horodok. This is a frightening, painful thought, and one that has haunted me for years. Many times, I myself don't believe that what I went through happened. It's as if it happened to someone else or didn't come to pass at all. If someone were to tell me all this, what really happened to me, I probably wouldn't believe it. It's a nightmare. It's unreal.

It's absolutely unreal.

I will not begin this account of my life by saying that I've forgiven and forgotten. I won't lie and say that the Holocaust is a distant memory in a far-off place, because, for me, it isn't. It's unforgivable that, in the twentieth century, civilized people did something like this. It's unforgivable that anything should ever happen like this—not just to the Jewish people, but any human race. And so, I live out my life carrying hateful memories of the Holocaust with no forgiveness in my heart.

But, despite this darkness, this pain of recalling my story, the joy I've received over the past decades compels me to share my experiences. The pleasant memories of my family—of being near my daughters and grandchildren, of making a home in Detroit, of having the chance to marry the man of my dreams—have readied me to face the past and record it, so that, when I'm gone, it will not be forgotten.

I am proud and grateful that my children and their children are all active in Holocaust survivor organizations around Detroit and have complete faith that they will continue to cultivate their legacy well into the future. My hope is that this book will help to keep my experiences alive and in the hearts of those dear to me, as well as reveal important family history that should be passed down.

In light of paying homage to the past and cultivating legacies, it seems logical to begin with a brief family history, starting with my father's side. My father was Beryl Gadziuk, and his father, Abba, was the only grandparent I knew. My grandfather was in my house nearly every day in my childhood. He had a beard and was religiously observant. He loved to hear me doing a blessing after dinner, taking pride in having me as a granddaughter. In fact, he'd always say I was his best granddaughter because I did so well in school.

Grandfather at one time lived with his wife, my grandmother, Tamara. I didn't know her well, because she was sick and always in bed, and died a few years before the war. After my grandmother died, my grandfather moved in with his youngest daughter, my aunt Dina (Gadziuk), who was married and had three children—two boys and a girl, my first cousins. Aunt Dina's husband was David, and they built a new house and also rented a house to an officer from the government for extra money. When the war came, Grandfather was killed in his mid-sixties.

In addition to Aunt Dina, my father had two brothers and another sister. His eldest brother was named Shevach, and Shevach and his family lived in a duplex with us when I was growing up. We lived in the front of the duplex, and they lived in the back. He was married to Brucha, and they had two sons and three daughters. The eldest son was good-looking, while the younger was sick all the time from tuberculosis.

Moshe was my father's next older brother, and he had a wife and two little girls. He lived a few blocks down the street from us. Father came next in line, then his sister Rifka. She moved to Detroit in the early 1920s with her husband, Morris Dowbrowitsky. The pair was very rich, because they owned a slaughterhouse in the Eastern Market. They had lots of property and had three children—two daughters and a son. After the war ended, Rifka's husband would often write letters and promise that he'd be like a father to me if I came to America. He didn't want me to move to Israel because I was the only one left—but more on that later.

My mother was Reizel Zietz, and her parents passed before I was born. Her mother was Basia, and her father was Shalom. I was named after my maternal grandmother, and had many cousins named Basia, as well. Most families on my mother's side, in fact, had a daughter named Basia and a son named Shalom.

Mother had four sisters and two brothers. Three of her siblings moved to America before I was born in 1924: Chana, Pesel, and Avramel (Abraham). Avramel moved to Detroit, Michigan with his wife, and later died in a car accident there, orphaning their two children. We all knew about this family in America in my early days, and so did our neighbors. They were jealous, because we had a connection to hopefully one day go to America, where we could have a home and place to work. We'd often get care packages from my aunts and uncle with powdered food and canned goods, while the family on my father's side would send us money for the holidays.

Mother's other brother, Meishel, was in Russia, married to a Jewish woman on the other side of the border. He had been planning on visiting us before the war broke out. Mother also had two other sisters, but I cannot remember their names.

This brings us, of course, to my family. My father Beryl and mother Reizel had me on November 27, 1924, and my brother, Sholom, a year and a half later. My given name was Basia (*Bash-ah*) Gadziuk. Basia is my

Yiddish name, and I later changed it to Beatrice when I came to America after the war ended.

It has been nearly eight decades since I was Basia Gadziuk, the little girl growing up in a small town near the Russian border, and over nine since the day Basia Gadziuk was born. At the time of this writing, I am ninety-three years old. For years and years after the Holocaust ended, it was very painful for me to look back and relive my experiences. Now that time has healed some of my wounds, now that I'm older, I am ready to open up. I hope that my descendants and those who come after them can use this story to stay strong in their heritage and better understand true struggle, fear, and loss—and also find the glimpses of sweet light and mercy that always emerge in the darkest of times.

Chapter One

I was born in David-Horodok (Davidgrudek), a small Jewish community in eastern Poland near the Russian border. Today, the small town is located in southern Belarus near the Ukranian border. Back then, the surrounding area was home to twenty to thirty thousand Jews, some Poles, and many Ukrainian citizens. It offered all the charms of small-town life while serving the nearby larger city of Pinsk. Most of the Jews lived in the center of town, while farmers lived on the outskirts. The Poles served in government positions, and other non-Jewish folks held positions in the City Hall, fire department, and police department. Two doctors held the fort in town—one a Ukrainian and the other Jewish, imported from Lodz. Many Jewish citizens worked in trades as tailors, carpenters, shoemakers, and other services. Other families, like my own, ran small businesses to account for their income. It was a busy life, but one that felt like home.

My father, a tall and straight man, ran a small, two-room grocery store a few blocks away from the center of the town. My mother helped him run the place, and, when I got old enough, I began to help out during the summer or school vacations. Most of our customers were Ukrainian and many of them bought on credit. We kept detailed records of people who hadn't paid, and some of them never did. We would sell food as well as cigarettes and tobacco, the latter of which my father would often get up in the middle of the night to smoke. Even though my mother did not smoke and he would've been angry with me if I'd tried it, my father's fingers were always brown from rolling the cigarettes.

He did very well as a business owner. He loved me very much and would always say that, one day, I'd marry an American and go to America. To marry an American was a good *shiddach*, a good match for a Jewish girl— maybe even the best one you could make. That was his dream for me, and he and mother started collecting things for my dowry. They began a collection of silverware, candlesticks, and the like for my future husband, hiding it in the floorboards of our house.

It helped, of course, that I'd stood out since birth with my shock of golden blonde hair, an unusual trait for a Jewish girl. This made me the object of attention early in life and gave my parents confidence that they'd find the right match for me when the time came.

In addition to helping my father with the store, my mother was a gifted seamstress. I would watch her take fabrics for coats and lay them across the table, marking them up with chalk and cutting through the threads with scissors. She had a sewing machine in the house and would sew my clothes. I thought that perhaps if she hadn't helped my father with the store, she could have become a fashion designer. She had a gift for making her own style, even though she'd never gone to school. While she tried to pass her talent to me, I found that I hated sewing. I learned how to use the machine, but certainly didn't enjoy it.

While we had a typical kosher, Yiddish-speaking family, our family was small compared to others in the town, which had many more children. Besides me, my younger brother Shalom was the only other child in the family. Shalom was a good-looking child, but he was a little prankster and we didn't get along. He used to throw the cat at me. He also wasn't very good in school, and my parents would often complain that he wasn't doing his homework, instead using his time to fool around.

Our house sat on a long road that led from the main street all the way to the Jewish cemetery. Every time there was a funeral, the procession would go right by our house down that street. Beyond the cemetery were farms. Our street was made up of all Jewish homes, and the houses had solid wood frames and floors that were very different from the awful housing in other parts of Poland. Our duplex had a living room, a kitchen, and one bedroom. I slept on the couch every night, and no one had their own bed. My brother slept with my father in the bedroom, which had two beds—the other belonging to my mother— and a wardrobe. We were also fortunate enough to have a porch and backyard, which helped the cramped living conditions seem a little larger.

It was a pleasant life, living in our duplex, despite having to deal with wood and coal stoves, which meant there was no easy way to heat the house in the winter. Similarly, water had to be brought in with buckets, and we used outhouses instead of toilets. We didn't even have a bathroom in the house. If you wanted to wash up, there was a big wash bucket in the yard. Transportation was far more difficult than it is today, since the train station was about five kilometers away and the only other modes of transportation were horses and wagons. But we didn't know any better, and we made do with what we had.

On hot days, we'd head to the beach close to our house. It sat on the edge of a lake and had beautiful white sand. I thoroughly enjoyed my time there, though my bright red two-piece bathing suit attracted a lot of attention. I'd often go there with my girlfriends, and all the boys would sit around us and talk. All the neighbors started gossiping about that, saying that Moisheach (the Messiah) was coming, because Moisheach would come whenever things happened that were out of the ordinary—like girls sitting amongst the boys in bathing suits. The Brodsky family, our neighbors, always sat at the window and spied on us when we went down to the water. They would tell my mother that I was down with the other girls among the boys, and she'd always reply that she could trust her daughter. Eventually, she told me what the Brodskys had been saying and what she'd been telling them in return. I wondered how much she *could* really trust me, since I was naïve in so many ways, and I never told her outright that she could trust me. It's something I wish I had said to her. I wish I had been more open with her.

To me, Pinsk—the biggest city in the area and only 60 miles to the west—was the end of the world.

There were five synagogues in David-Horodok, and, in each, men and women would sit separately. That meant I'd sit upstairs with my mother while my father and brother sat downstairs. In our synagogue, the *rabbi* was Moishela, a handsome younger man. The *rebetzin*, the wife of the rabbi, was a nice woman. The pair had beautiful children, between five and ten years old.

In addition to devoutly going to the synagogue each week, we observed other religious practices. One experience in particular that stands out in my mind is visiting the *mikveh* with my mother when I was twelve or thirteen. The *mikveh* is a purification bath, and since we had no running water in the house, I wasn't used to taking baths too often—maybe once a week or so. I was taught to dip my head in the pool three times as a woman sat there and said, "Kosher, kosher, kosher." My mother took me there only once, to show me what it was like, even though she went there herself every month.

Every Friday evening, we had a Shabbat dinner, the Jewish Sabbath dinner. My mother would make *cholent*, a traditional Jewish stew with potatoes and meat, every Friday in preparation for the Sabbath. Since chicken was a delicacy, we usually had beef in our *cholent*. During the week, we would simply eat vegetables, potatoes, rice, and noodles. Shabbat dinner was mostly with the immediate family, but sometimes my grandfather would also attend. Shabbat was also the only day off we had from school, which made it a special occasion. For the holidays, my mother baked her own *challah*—a special bread—and cakes. She was a very good cook.

We followed many holiday traditions. On Yom Kippur, we would fast. On Sukkot, my uncle would build a *sukkah*—a makeshift hut—in the backyard. Chanukah was also a minor holiday, where we would light candles and play with dreidels. On Purim, my mom would make *hamantashen*—filled triangular-shaped cookies—and we would do a play in school. On Pesach, we would have *seders*, feasts. I remember we would open the door for Elihu Hanavi and read the Haggadah late into the night. We also made our own *matzah*, unleavened bread, for Pesach. Several families would get together and partner up to make the *matzah*. Shavuot was a happy holiday, and we would go visit each other during it.

I belonged to the Shomer Haleumi, one of the two youth Zionist organizations. We had a board and a president, and we would hold meetings to talk about going to Israel—a goal that the organization taught us to strive for, since Israel held the Holy Land. Friday nights, we would have dancing events and dance the *horah*. We played ping pong there as well.

The Shomer also used to have Kinus conventions, where they organized trips for us to go to a nearby city for a small vacation. They arranged to have a steam river boat transport us to Stolin, Pinsk, and other cities, and people from those cities would let us stay with them for a while. My father occasionally paid for me to go on these trips, especially at my mother's urging. She probably saw that I was naïve and quiet, and I knew she wanted me to be with people and be more outgoing. When I first signed up, I was the first one picked and went with my host family to their large, rich house in Stolin. They brought me a glass of milk and chocolate, the latter of which I had never tasted before. The next time, I went to Pinsk. I felt like I was going to a big city each time, especially since I was only twelve or thirteen years old.

Chapter Two

Unlike my mother, who never went to school, my brother and I were able to attend a private school in town called the Jewish Tarbut school. It had few Polish influences outside its national program, and heavily focused on Hebrew. My parents could have sent me and my brother to the Polish public school, where they wouldn't have had to pay tuition, but, like most Jewish families in our community, they were adamant that we attend the Tarbut school. This was because the Tarbut school was one of the best Tarbut schools in all of Poland, and its teachers and other involved individuals were very committed to conservative Jewish beliefs.

Even the director of the school himself, Avresha Olshanski, was very Zionistic. That meant that he was in favor of the re-establishment of the Jewish homeland (Holy Land) in Israel. To this end, he heavily encouraged students to speak only Hebrew, which meant I had to stop speaking Yiddish and start focusing on my studies as soon as possible. Since I was also part of Shomer Haleumi, the exploration of my Jewish history and heritage became very important to me.

Eventually, I took pride in being at the top of my class, and history was my favorite subject. All the teachers liked me, and I used to remember everything they taught me about history—dates, times, whatever was written for the exam. My favorite teacher was named Ehrich, and he taught history. Often, the teacher would pick on me to answer a question about this war or that war, and I always knew the answer. We learned both Polish and Jewish history, and my dream was to become a Hebrew teacher and emigrate to Israel. Most of my peers also wanted to go to Palestine, and there were regular lotteries for the older girls to get certificates to live in the *kibbitzuim* and then move to Palestine. One of the girls who lived across the street from us went this route. I hoped to join her and the others one day.

Speaking and writing Hebrew came easily to me, and I joined a club—the B'nei Yehudah club—that took these talents very seriously. Avresha Olashanski was the one who had organized this club, and to join we had to give an oath to only speak Hebrew at all times: *ach v'rak b'ivrit,* "only in Hebrew." In fact, some students from this group would often spy on club members to see if we weren't speaking Hebrew, even at home. We didn't dare speak Yiddish anywhere, which meant our parents couldn't understand us. I'd often have to show my parents what I meant by pointing or gesturing, afraid that I'd be caught if I uttered any words in Yiddish. My brother, since he was younger than me, didn't join the club. That made me the only person in my family to speak Hebrew in the house. Eventually, because of this club and the Tarbut school, David-Horodok began to be called the "Tel-Aviv of Polesye," the Tel-Aviv of Poland, due to all the Hebrew speakers. A lot of parents and community members also learned Hebrew because of our influence.

Our parents paid 20 zlotys per month for my brother and me to attend the school, which was a lot of money for them. It was used to keep the school running and pay its teachers. The building was only a few blocks from my house, but we had to be careful when we walked to it because it was near the outskirts of town, where most of the non-Jewish population lived. As much as we tried to avoid them, I do remember walking to school and often running into Ukrainian boys who threw stones at us because we were Jewish. I was afraid that they would beat me up and tried to steer clear of them most days. I'd even seen my parents and other families lock up their houses around Christmastime each year, because some of the non-Jewish people would get drunk and try to break through our windows. There were slogans and signs to not buy from Jewish people. Aside from our little haven in the center of town, very few Polish people lived in our town—except for the officers and government employees. The rest were Ukranian, and some often came to trade their crops and buy from my parents' store.

The school itself was, as I recall, five separate buildings that took up about an acre. Boys and girls learned a variety of subjects together, like Hebrew, Polish, math, science, Jewish and Polish history, and geography. There were about twenty-five kids in my grade, and the girls outnumbered the boys. A lot of students dropped out after fifth grade for reasons I don't know. That didn't stop me from making a lot of friends—nearly ten girls who I was in a clique with. We were always together. Looking back, I had a beautiful social life. I was part of a lot of clubs, and we'd play ping pong and dance and just have fun together. It was really nice.

My mother would give me a nickel sometimes, so I could go to the bakery across from the school during lunchtime and buy a *pletzlach*—a coffee cake—to eat. The ones with poppy seeds were my favorite. I would join the cluster of other children during lunchtime at 11:30 a.m. and walk across the street to get this delicious goodie, then make my way back to the school to finish the day promptly at 3 p.m. The baker had a son named Monia Bregman, who, I was told, survived in Russia and eventually went to Israel after the war.

I first heard a few of my peers mention Hitler as I neared the eighth grade. They said that Hitler was going to come in 1938 or 1939. I didn't know who or what Hitler was, because I was too young. But the other students were older, and they knew what was coming. I don't particularly remember my parents ever discussing it, and I didn't really pay attention to the details. It was very easy to stay isolated in our little town, since we didn't have any connection to the outside world. Only the rich people had radios.

The Aronkin family was one such family who had a radio. They owned a leather factory and sold leather, which made them one of the richest families in town—along with the Finkelsteins. I got to know them well when I was fourteen, because their son Isa Aronkin had a crush on me. He was dating my girlfriend Freidel Debroshin, and I didn't think it'd be nice of him to break up with her just to date me, so when he asked me to go out with him I said no. Even so, he did keep us updated on what he heard on the radio after the war began. Some evenings, we'd get together so he could tell us what he'd heard about the Germans, Russians, and chaos. Both he and Freidel were later killed.

At that time, though, what was happening outside my little existence was nothing compared to my graduation. In 1939, I completed the eighth grade at fourteen years old. Little did I know that my small, naïve world was about to get a lot bigger—and crueler.

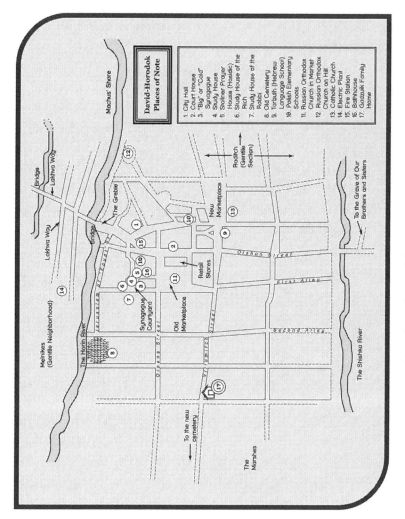

Map of David-Horodok and places of note.

Chapter Three

When the war broke out on September 1, 1939, Nazi Germany took over half of Poland while the other half fell to the Russians. Nearly overnight, everything changed. We all became a part of Russia on September 19, 1939. I even had a Russian passport with my picture on it. The Tarbut school closed down, and I had to go back to seventh grade at the public Russian school. One day, they showed a movie outside on the wall. It was a silent movie with subtitles I couldn't read, because everything looked upside down and foreign. I thought to myself, *Oh, God. I went to school all these years and now I can't read!* Thus, my days of speaking and writing only in Hebrew drew to a close. All my teachers came from Russia, and I learned Russian. To my surprise, I loved learning the language. We learned history, language, math, geography—and we even had physics, which I could never really grasp.

The high school was mixed, which meant I was going to school with more than just my little Jewish clique. All of my old Jewish teachers were gone, too. My new physics teacher had a big belly. My new history teacher later dated a Russian nurse and they had a child together. It was all different, but I tried to stay on top of my studies and continue learning as much as I could.

There were, of course, much less pleasant changes. Within three days of the Russians' arrival, my father lost his business. While we were allowed to stay in our homes so long as we didn't defy the Communist rules, small stores ceased to exist as the government took control of everything. The wealthy families that owned large businesses were immediately packed off to Siberia or similar barren places, along with anti-Communists, Zionists, or religious factions. It was a deep shock when my best friend Sarah Finkelstein told me that her father had disappeared to an unknown place. He had been the owner of the leather factory.

Once a small business owner, my father was forced to work in a job involving barges on the river. The paychecks were miserable, not even enough to feed a family, and everyone I knew was in the same position. My father's new workplace was not far away, so I would bring him his lunch each day. It was just enough to keep him going. Food was scarce and rationed by the Russians. In the beginning, we still had food and would trade dry goods for clothes or shoes or other things. Later, we joined the long lines of people who needed bread, sugar, and other foods from the distribution center. Communist speakers flooded the area with their propaganda, but people didn't care so much about that. We needed food, and announcements of food distributions had us scrambling to get our meager share.

One night, I snuck out of the house very early to reach a sugar distribution center before the others rushed in. I wanted to show my parents that I could contribute something to the house. I got there early enough and had to wait in line for most of the night until they opened the store in the morning. My efforts were rewarded with a bag of wet, lumpy sugar and a severe scolding from my father, who was more than a little upset that I'd gone to the store by myself. After that, he restricted me from any future attempts.

Despite the occupation in 1939 and the hard times that followed, I matured mentally as well as physically into young womanhood. I began to enjoy the Russian scene, although I didn't agree with the Communistic theology. The Russian school made me appreciate Russian culture, just like the Tarbut school had made me appreciate Hebrew and Jewish culture. I learned more about Russian music, dancing, and language, and it was all fascinating to me. It opened up a whole new world. There was also little trouble from the occupying Russian soldiers, despite all that has been said about them running wild. In my experience, they were a lively bunch who loved to sing and dance, and, overall, they were exuberant.

It was around this time that I had my first romantic experience. Apparently, I had become an attractive young lady, even as a teenager at the age of fifteen. On a bright day, a girlfriend and I were walking on the only decent road in town when we bumped into two soldiers walking the opposite way. As they passed, one of the soldiers glanced at me and my heart flipped. He was so handsome! I thought, *If he would want to date me, I'd be the happiest girl.* Sure enough, the next day, he looked me up. His name was Beryl Kolodny. He was a Jewish soldier, a veteran from the Polish army who was now drafted into the Russian Armed Forces. While he was twenty-four and I was just fifteen, I was immediately enamored.

He spotted me at one of the dances we went to at the courtyard near the church, the local hotspot for a lot of teenagers and young people. There'd often be a five- or six-piece band that played for our enjoyment, and I was a natural at dancing. I'd picked it up on my own. So, when Beryl asked me to dance—I think it was a waltz—I didn't hesitate. My affection for him only grew as he walked me home, and we sat on the porch of my house to talk until early morning. My parents undoubtedly noticed us out there, but they never said anything to me about it.

Beryl wanted to marry me, but the only thing I knew about marriage was that you had a small ceremony and went over to City Hall to seal the deal. He'd ask me many times over to get married throughout the course of our relationship, but we never did. We did date until he was called back to the army, when the Germans came in. I walked with him to the Russian disbursement base the very next day, tearfully bidding him farewell. Little did I know, I would never see him again. He never came back to David-Horodok, and he didn't go to Israel to find his sister, who had gone to live in a *kibbutz* before the war. Later, I found out he was killed in action when the Nazis turned on Russia.

My other memorable romantic experience was a bit less conventional. When my father worked with the barges, I would take the same path every day to bring him lunch. The road passed by a partitioned prisoners' camp, and one day I saw a note sticking through the wires. Curious, I took the note and read the scrawled Russian lettering.

How beautiful you are, and I notice you as you pass by every day. What a delight to just see you.

-Vavya

The next day, I found a similar note. I could never see the prisoners clearly, so I had no idea who was sending me these little love letters. Eventually, they stopped, because the prisoner was gone. The notes had such beautiful handwriting and were so beautifully composed that I felt bad to simply tear them up, so instead I treasured them. My family had an embroidered velvet pillow decorated with flowers that sat on the bed, so I stuck the letters inside it for safekeeping. Unfortunately, my little brother liked to spy on me, and he saw me hide the letters. He told my father, and I received a stern lecture and was forced to tear them up. My father was especially disturbed because "Vavya", the name at the end of each note, was not exactly a Jewish name.

Our time under the Russians was difficult, but I was young and adapted. While I lived contently for a couple years, difficulty became disaster in 1941, when the German Nazi Army broke its pact with the Soviet Russian regime and attacked it with full force. At first, we waited while they plowed through larger cities, wreaking havoc upon anyone and everyone. But it would only be a matter of time before they came to David-Horodok and some of the greatest tragedies of my life unfolded.

Chapter Four

In August of 1941, the German soldiers came into town. Before we fully realized what was happening, the Nazis were in our backyards. Two soldiers stopped my father on the street one day, and one of the soldiers—his name was Karl Ludwig—gave him a pack of cigarettes and the address of his mother in Vienna. "Hitler's aim is to wipe out all the Jewish people," he said. "But I feel sorry for your pretty, young daughter. Here is the address of my mother in Vienna. Your daughter should take the train and go there. Don't tell anyone she is Jewish. My mother will keep her."

The six-foot-two soldier continued to call on us for three days, always paying me special attention. He would bring cigarettes for my father each time, along with the same warning for me: "You need to leave. Hitler is coming."

On the third day, he called on our house with his helmet under his arm. He'd come to say goodbye to me and my father, but only I was awake. We conversed in German. I didn't know the language well, but I understood a little bit. "I don't want to fight," he said. "But I have an order to move on, so that's what I have to do."

When he left, the neighbors came over and asked what he'd said to me. I told them what he'd explained about Hitler, and how he wanted me to run away before bad things happened to the Jews. They all shrugged and said, "Oh, that will never happen."

Everyone was terrified when the Germans began weeding out the men and boys to be sent away, supposedly to work. We knew that there was a great possibility we'd never see those who were chosen again, especially after what had happened to the wealthy families when the Russians had made them disappear. The German soldiers went from house to house, dragging out everyone they selected. When they stopped by our house, my father and brother were in the bedroom, so the soldiers didn't see them and left empty-handed.

But the Ukrainians who lived in David-Horodrok—referred to as Horodtchukas—wanted the city to be purged of Jews so they could take whatever wealth we still had hidden in our homes, and they knew that the Germans had missed some of us in their search. They even went so far as to spread rumors that the Jews had cut the telephone lines and were waiting on the Russians to come in and save them. Soon after, the German soldiers came back and marched through the town again, rounding up more men and children with the Horodtchukas' help.

Although they tried to hide, my father and brother were seized and forced from our home. As my father struggled against his captors, a German soldier put a pistol to his head and shot him in cold blood. I was there when it happened, in the house with my mother. As the shot echoed through the town, thudding through my ribcage like an irregular heartbeat, I ran out of the house to find my father lying in a pool of blood. It was raining. I'd never seen so much rain in my life. Torrents of water soaked me through and pelted my father's unmoving body. I began to hemorrhage, throwing up blood as it ran from my mouth and nose at the same time. I couldn't even scream. I lost my voice, my words, and just kept throwing up. I was in a daze, a nightmare I couldn't escape. I could never begin to describe the agony and terror I felt, though the memory is still vividly and frighteningly clear to me today.

It must have been ten or fifteen minutes before the Hordotchukas came by again, triumphant as they began kicking the women, disabled, elderly, and remaining children from the town. They threatened us with sticks and yelled at us to move fast. It continued to pour as we left behind my parents' precious dowry collection that they'd hidden in the cellar for my future husband—a silver candelabra, dry goods, shoes, coats, and blankets—and all the pleasant memories of our little duplex. We left in what we were wearing, skirts and blouses. We didn't take anything with us, except for my brother's heavy winter jacket. My mother grabbed it on our way out the door and wrapped me up in it.

We left my father in the backyard with a blanket over his body. My uncle Shevach and his older son Laizel had been taken away with the other men, and my grandfather was with one of his granddaughters, so I didn't know what had happened to him. Later, I would come to find out that my uncle, cousin, and those other men—all Jewish males over the age of fourteen—had been summoned to the marketplace that day. They had been told to take shovels with them, having been promised to get work that day. The marketplace had been surrounded by German SS troops and Hordotchukas, who'd led the group of men to a close-by village, and they had been shot to death there. They were thrown into mass graves by the Hordotchukas, who stole all the gold rings, watches, clothing, shoes, gold teeth, and other belongings of the deceased. They didn't even wait to make sure the Jews were dead before they started burying them. Some were buried alive.

Other men had tried to make their way out of the town with the women and children. There was a rabbi—Rabbi Moshele—who'd bought a house close to us, from people who had emigrated to Palestine. I'd been in his house before to buy yeast that his wife was selling. He had a beautiful wife and kids and was a nice-looking man himself. He'd dressed in women's clothing to try and escape David-Horodok, but the Hordotchukas had recognized him as he walked out of town. He and the other disguised men had been brutally beaten and thrown from a bridge into the river. Very few had escaped.

These were the fates my father had been hiding from when his efforts were foiled. My brother had been hiding with my father, and he'd been seized as well. We found his body on our way out of town, face down in the grass in a bare space between some houses. Shevach's wife covered him with a blanket, and my mother pushed me onward.

No one seemed to care where we went, so we walked south out of town. As we walked away from what remained of David-Horodok, a

Hordotchuka played the accordion—happy music as we marched toward more suffering. My mother decided we'd go to Sarny, a city about 100 kilometers south of David-Horodok, where she had a cousin who might be able to help us. When we passed by the outskirts of town, we ran across the graves. All the men and boys the soldiers had collected had been killed and piled up in holes they'd dug themselves. No male over the age of fourteen had been spared.

It continued to rain as we left the town, soaking us through and exhausting us, but I said nothing. It was like someone had taken away my tongue, and I didn't even have the energy to feel afraid. What was there to be afraid of, anyway? I'd just seen the worst horrors imaginable take place right outside my childhood home. That night, when it got too dark to see anymore, we collapsed onto the wet grass and slept. I heard that some Ukrainian men later came and took the young girls they could find, raping them in the fields as the others slept. My brother's jacket may have saved me from that atrocity. Wrapped up in it and sleeping, I must have looked like an old woman.

The city was weeks away on foot, and we'd have to stop in many towns along the way. Thankfully, in each town, there was a Jewish social organization that would spare us some food and shelter for the night. The next morning, we'd move on, aiming for the next town. We walked through Stolin, then Virsostz, then Dumbrovatsya. My voice did not return, not for a long time.

After weeks of walking, we finally arrived in Sarny with the small group of people we'd traveled with. Slowly, our group began to disperse as people found their families in different parts of the town. In Sarny, Jews had been left to stay in their homes, although the Ukrainians had been given the right to plunder all their assets for a few days and no one stopped them. My mother had two cousins in the city, and they tried to help us the best they could. But, in addition to food being scarce, they didn't have enough room to house both of us together. The only solution was to have me sleep in one cousin's house, and my mother to stay at the other cousin's home.

I stayed with my cousin Arnold Frumin's parents. I still remember meeting Arnold for the first time. He was five years old and very cute. His family owned a material store—a fabric store—that was a good business in Poland. His parents, my mother's cousins, were named Victor and Dreizel. Victor's younger brother, Meyer, who was thirteen at the time of the war, ultimately survived by hiding in a Gentile's farm and tending their sheep. Meyer later became a dentist in America. My mother stayed with her cousin Brucha, who had three boys. One of the boys, named Zalman, was sent to Russia to work and presumably died in the labor force there. Another one of Brucha's sons escaped to Israel. The last was killed in the ghetto that later formed in Sarny.

I was still able to see my mother every day, since the houses were just a few blocks from each other. There was a *zalman*, a single man, staying at the same house as my mother. He would come out and talk to me occasionally about school and Israel. I never said much during our conversations. I was very depressed after what happened to my father and brother. I was in shock. I didn't talk, and I couldn't stand when I heard people talking. Instead, I would walk away and stay secluded. These days, they probably would've sent me to a psychiatrist. My mother, on the other hand, was incredibly brave. She saw that I was sick, that I was a changed person. She kept to herself and never mentioned my father's or brother's names, even though I knew she was hurting just as much as I was.

It would be years before I realized that we weren't the only ones who didn't want to talk about it.

For a whole year, my mother was able to provide food for the both of us by trading her skill at sewing with a Ukrainian widow. We coexisted with the Ukrainians for a little more than a year, but, in the spring of 1942, we were uprooted again when the Germans formed a ghetto in Sarny to isolate all the Jews and keep them imprisoned.

A close-up view of the towns of David-Horodok and Sarny.

30

Chapter Five

The ghetto in Sarny was packed with people, and we had to fit several families into one house. My mother continued to stay with her one cousin, while I moved into a three-room house with Arnold and his family, along with three other families. There was very little food, and many times my mother would hide her bread so I could have some when I visited her. We had one bathroom for everyone to use, and people just tried to live day-by-day to make it through.

There were new rules in the ghetto to further separate us from the town itself. The Germans had formed a *Judenrat*, a Jewish council that had to meet their demands in order to not be hurt or killed by Hitler's authorities. They commanded that we wear yellow emblems bearing the Star of David over our hearts. Our houses also had to have a Star of David drawn on them. We had a curfew, and couldn't be out of our houses past 8 p.m. There were wires surrounding the ghetto, and we weren't allowed to leave most of the time. Police guarded the gate, both Ukrainian and German soldiers.

Sometimes, we'd have to work for our allowance of bread each day or give great quantities of gold or the clothes off our backs to the Germans. Several times, I went to dig ditches somewhere outside the ghetto with other young people. We thought that, if we gave everything that was demanded of us, we'd be allowed to live—though we heard more and more of ghettos around the country being liquidated, their inhabitants killed or driven off to unknown places.

Around that time, I made a friend named Miriam. Her father was a *shochet*, one who supervised the kosher slaughter of cows and chickens. One day, she told me that there were rumors of my cousin, Victor Frumin, building a shelter in case our ghetto was liquidated.

"Are the rumors true?" she asked. "If they are, will you please take me with you?"

I frowned, because Victor had never said a word of it to me even though we lived in the same house. I thought it impossible that he'd keep that secret from me. "Don't you think I would know if he was building a shelter?"

After about ten months, the Germans began to call and count everyone, then would send the people back to their homes no worse for wear. It confused us and worried us. Who knew when they were going to complete the liquidation and kill us all off? They wanted to mislead people, because they were afraid we might fight back. After about a month, they took several hundred people away to work. No one knew where they actually went, and this made us even more nervous. Finally, they called us a third time, ordering us to meet at a specific spot at 8 a.m. the following morning—August 26, 1942. Everyone expected the worst at this point, and most of us were up the whole night, afraid this might be our last night on earth.

That morning, I woke up as usual and got dressed. The Germans walked through our ranks, herding us and shouting for us to hurry up. Everyone, mostly the women and children who were left, was guarded by the soldiers. They began to march away, and I felt compelled to follow them and find my mother as quickly as possible. I spotted her in the crowd and reached out to touch her when someone pulled on the back of my collar.

"Don't follow her. You'll never come back." It was Victor Frumin, the cousin I'd lived with for so many months. He grabbed me and led me through the rising confusion of the crowd, stopping in the field at the back of his house.

He pointed toward the cellar, which he'd covered with dirt and a double wall. "Come on. You go in there."

"No, I want to go and find my mother," I told him. My mother was all alone in the crowd, and I felt guilty I'd left her that way. All the families were gathered together, and I was not with her.

"You need to go in the cellar," he insisted.

He must have realized that I was a child who didn't fully understand what was going on, because he grabbed me by the back of my collar again and pushed me into the cellar in front of him, locking the door behind us.

I never saw my mother again.

I did not see what happened to my mother, but my third cousin Harold Perlstein lived in Sarny at the same time we did. He had a wife named Miriam and a child, and I only saw him a couple times and never talked to him. He'd been born in a village near Sarny and then moved to the city. His father had died young, and his mother was crippled, perhaps from polio. He had three sisters and one brother.

Harold had lived in Sarny much longer than us, and when the liquidation came about, he witnessed what happened that day. The following chapter is in his words, taken from the Sarny Yizkor Book and translated from Yiddish. It covers the beginning of the ghetto formation to the end of many lives—likely including my mother's and my other cousins'.[1]

---

1. https://www.jewishgen.org/Yizkor/sarny/sar305.html

Chapter Six
The Sarny Ghetto: The Beginning of the End

By Harold Perlstein

The Germans occupied Sarny in July 1941. The first thing they did was commandeer fifty Jews to work in the warehouses, issuing an order that if anything happened to a German, these fifty Jews would be put to death.

In the first days, the Germans permitted the Ukrainians to plunder Jewish assets. In the following three days and three nights, the Ukrainians in Sarny and its vicinity did exactly that. Nobody stood in their way. After those three days, the Germans drove the Ukrainians away, and stopped the plunder.

At the end of July 1941, the German military demanded the creation of a *Judenrat*. They demanded of the former president of the Sarny community that he place himself at the head of the *Judenrat*. Not taking note of the fact that he was already seventy years old, he assumed this obligation against his own will to manage the *Judenrat* and fulfill all the demands of the Hitler authorities. The *Judenrat* was composed of the following five Jews: The President (seventy-year-old Gerszunok), Vice-President (Kantorowicz), Secretary (Neiman), and Treasurer (Grossman and Pickman jointly). The first demand was that all Jews must wear white bands on their right arms with a Star of David sewn on it, and all Jewish houses must have a Star of David drawn on them. If this order was not carried out, the authorities imposed a fine of thirty rubles and murderously beat the offender. It was the Ukrainian police who were mostly involved with this.

On August 15, a month after the capture of Sarny, the German authorities levied a demand on the Jewish community for a contribution of thirteen kilograms of gold. This had to be accomplished in the course of eight days. Every day, the authorities took 400 Jews to do labor. They had to saw wood and build bridges over the Sluch River to replace the ones the Russians had destroyed, dig peat, etc. The women carried bricks from one end of the city to the other. Workers received one hundred grams of bread a day. Part of the Jews lived off stores they had from before the war. Others bartered with the peasants, giving away their best possessions for a bit of bread, and the largest part hungered. Through the *Judenrat*, the German authorities began to confiscate Jewish assets: cattle, horses, radios, furniture, bedding, etc. The President, Gerszunok, would shout: "Jews, give everything that is demanded of you, and they will let you live. 'A cow that is milked will not be slaughtered.'"

On the eve of Yom Kippur 1941, a new demand arrived: in place of the armbands, all Jews will have to wear yellow emblems on their back and over their heart. These emblems were to be eight centimeters in length. The authorities issued an order that all the Jews, on Yom Kippur, should assemble at a place near the city. At that time, a frightful panic erupted among the Jews. We understood what they wanted to do with us. But whether they wanted to or not, all the Jews, wearing the yellow insignia, came to the designated location on Yom Kippur.

All the Jews turned over their gold watches to the Gebiets-Kommissar, golden feathers, etc. Then, all the Jews were registered, men and women. The younger ones were sent off to do work in the city, and the older ones, for the time being, were released to return home.

For the time being, the day ended only with fright.

Then the harsh winter of 1941 set in. During the month of October, an order came from the authorities that the Jews had to turn over fur coats and boots for the army, and so the Jews gave away their fur coats and boots. Apart from this, it was demanded that we sew new coats and boots for the army.

A number of quiet months passed, and we all thought we would be able to live peacefully. Suddenly, a fresh tragedy: In January 1942, an order arrived that every Jew had to pay up a contribution of seven grams of gold per capita. As there were five thousand Jews in our city, it was necessary to pay in thirty-five kilograms of gold. This was a massive tragedy, because among us were many Jews who had fled to us from other cities after 1939, and it wasn't possible to demand anything from them.

Accordingly, it was very difficult. But seeing that we had a good relationship with the Gebiets-Kommissar—he would say that the Sarny Jews were good ones, they would not be "made kaput"—he deferred the contribution for several months. A little at a time, with a great deal of trouble and suffering, the contribution was paid off. And so, with troubles, with hunger, and with cold, with great need and pain, whoever sustained themselves and whoever didn't, managed to survive the severe winter.

In the month of April, a fresh decree arrived: A ghetto was to be created for the Jews in the course of fifteen days. The Jews themselves must divide off several back streets of the city and cordon them off with boards. Then, the terror began. The Jews left their homes, and everyone ran, as if fleeing a fire, into the ghetto. At the same time, a Jewish police force was set up, with the commandant Margolis at its head. Their mission was to maintain order in the ghetto, stand at the gates, and not permit Jews to leave the ghetto—and not permit Ukrainians and Poles within. Jews were permitted to leave the ghetto only through the gate, in accordance with a special permit from the police commandant. If a Jew was caught outside the ghetto without such a permit, he was punished with a monetary fine and a murderous beating. There was an instance that a woman went out of the ghetto without a permit. She was caught, and she and her entire family, consisting of seven people, were shot the same day.

In addition to this, the Germans began to bring people into the ghetto from the surrounding villages. The Germans took everything away from them. News arrived that Jews were being killed in Rivne, Kovel, and other cities around Sarny. The situation grew more critical and worse every day. Hunger began, accompanied by death from hunger. We saw that the catastrophe was unavoidable for us as well.

It was at that time that I had concluded with my comrades and neighbors to stage an assault, burn down the city, and flee to the forests. Many were of the same mind as me, and a portion were opposed. They said that one should not summon the wolf out of the forest if he does not come of his own volition. And in many places, the ghettos had already been liquidated. They argued that it would not come to that with us, because we went to work, and we paid all of the contributions, but we must be ready for any circumstance. Should the day arrive—God forbid—we should be organized, be able to mount a resistance, and not allow ourselves to be led off like sheep to the slaughter, as it had occurred in other cities.

Indeed, we had begun to organize ourselves. This became known to the Jewish Police Commandant, Margolis, and he was not opposed to it. He said: "Keep yourselves strong, friends! We will not allow ourselves to be stabbed like calves." One time, while sitting with the president of the *Judenrat*, Gerszunok, who was a neighbor of mine, we conversed about the sorrowful end of all the cities around Sarny. When I secretly approached him about the organization of a resistance, Gerszunok replied: "You don't have to tell me anything but do as you find it necessary to do." From his answer, I understood that he agreed with us. This bolstered our work to make ourselves ready, and the entire city of Jews was taken with the thought of declaring war on the murderers.

We were in the ghetto from April until August 1942. On the 23rd of August, the terrifying days of the liquidation of the ghetto commenced. The Ukrainian police encircled the ghetto, the Jewish police were no longer given access to the guard posts, and no one was taken out of the ghetto to go to work. We understood that this was the last of our days, and we no longer had anything to lose. The time for vengeance had come.

On Wednesday, the 24th of August, almost all of the Jews in our ghetto gathered together in the *Judenrat*. We divided the men up into groups of fifty, with a group leader at the head. Each group had a mission to carry out. We had provisioned grenades, caustic soda to burn out the eyes, and benzene, gas to set the city on fire, and we waited for an order.

The chief commander of the day was Police Commandant Margolis. We received an order from the Germans that, on Thursday, August 25, all the Jews must present themselves at the ghetto gate, and each family would be called out of the ghetto in alphabetical order. We received this order on Wednesday. We had until early Thursday morning to get everything ready.

However, here, the secretary of the *Judenrat*, Neiman, stood up against us. He explained to the gathering that we were not being called to be killed, but only to select out healthy men for work. The people permitted themselves to be misled by him and did nothing. We also received an order from Commandant Margolis that we should not take matters into our own hands but wait for Thursday.

On the night of Wednesday into Thursday, we did not sleep at all. We got iron [tools] ready and sat ready at the door to await the murderers. In this way, the night passed in fear, thinking about our end. On Thursday, August 25, at 6 a.m., people began to arrive at the ghetto gate. When 300 people had gathered, they were taken away. Within the ghetto, Ukrainian police circulated and looked into the houses. Jews who had not left the houses were shot by the police. Many Jews committed suicide out of panic, using poison.

In this manner, my family too was taken out: my mother, my sister Sarah with two children, my second sister Toiba with two children, myself, my wife and child, uncles, aunts, brothers-in-law, sisters-in-law, and male and female cousins. We were all taken over to the second side, to a place ringed with two rows of barbed wire. There was a distance of one meter between the two barbed wire fences. In between the two fences, German and Ukrainian police circulated. When someone got close to the fence, they shot them to death. Two machine guns were set up near the gate of the ghetto. When we were brought to the camp, Jews from the surrounding villages and towns were already inside: Dąbrowica, Bereznica, Rokitno, Klesów… in total, 14,000 Jews.

I complained to Margolis about the fact that he had promised we would not let ourselves be stabbed like calves, and how, in the end, he had not let us carry out our pre-planned attack. He answered: "It is lost, and this is our fate. What were we to do? Flee, save ourselves, and leave our wives and children in the hands of the murderers who would cut them to pieces? It is better that all of us go into the pit together!" These were his last words.

While there, I encountered one of my brothers, with a wife and four children, brought from Klesów. The entire family lay and waited for a terrifying death. It was intensely hot, and people fainted from thirst. For a small bottle of water, gold watches and gold rings were given away to the Ukrainian police. Paper money was torn up and thrown into the toilets out of fear of having money in one's possession.

On August 25, at two o'clock in the afternoon, all of the residents of Rokitno were called out of the camp. Five hundred came out. Immediately at the gate, their bundles were taken away, along with everything they had. Everything was loaded onto wagons, which had been readied for this purpose at the gate. A kilometer from the camp, there was a small forest in which three large pits had been dug. The Germans led away the victims, the first 500, and ordered them to undress and lie down in the pit. The murderers shot them there.

I stood there like that and tried to manage our hopeless situation with friends. Suddenly, I saw people running, and the barbed wire fence was breached. This jolted me like an electric shock: *Run*! I did not understand what or where, but only that it was necessary to run. I left my friend Vartszun standing and began to run, forgetting that I had a wife and child. When I ran over the barbed wire, there had already accumulated a mound—a meter high—of dead people, wounded people, and people who had fainted. They'd fallen from the shooting of the German and Ukrainian gendarmerie. I also saw that the barracks, full of people, were burning. It was the Germans who had fired them.

I ran, coursing over the piles of the dead bodies. Bullets whistled by my ears. Grenades fell. It was a fire and a hell on all sides. I ran at that time, but I did not know what I was doing. When I found myself about 400 meters from the camp, I heard the voice of my sister Toiba. She was running after me, and shouted, "Stop, wait! Let us not get separated! Let us run together!" When we came to the first street of the city, the bandits blocked our way. We lost one another. Toiba ran into the house of a Pole, and I, along with two other Jews, leapt into a Pole's attic. There was a bit of straw there in which we hid, lying down. Ten minutes later, we heard that the Germans were going through the houses searching. A Polish woman had said, "Here, in the stall. Three Jews have hidden themselves." The Germans came into the stall and began to shout. We did not reply, and they went away. Many Jews were found in the pens, orchards, and gardens, and shot on the spot. An hour later, the Ukrainians came to search in the stall and up in the attic. However, thanks to the fact that we had hidden ourselves in the straw, they didn't find us. At about midnight, when we heard the shooting and explosions lessen, all three of us tore off the side of the roof and crawled out of the attic.

The night was bright, and it was the fourteenth day of Elul. We crossed over many dead bodies that lay in the gardens. Through back alleys, over fences and gates, we exited the city, reached the Sluch River, and walked the entire night along the edge of the river until we reached the village of Lyukhcha, seven kilometers from Sarny.

Here, our situation again became serious. We did not know what to do, where to put ourselves. We feared the sunshine, and even our own shadows. We trembled, fearing that, at any instant, the bandits would seize us again. Mr. Olshansky said to me, "Let us throw ourselves into the river and drown!"

I replied, "No! If I have saved myself from the murderers, am I to drown myself now? I've got time to wait for that!"

A difference of opinion arose among us. I wanted to go into the village, and the other two of my friends wanted to go into the forest. And so, indeed, they did go off to the forest, thinking that they would be able to conceal themselves better there. I went to the village of Stril's'k, because I knew some people there. In the village, I hid out among the peasants for a long period of time, suffering mightily from want and cold, contracting all manner of diseases. In the end, I saw that I would not be able to hold out there. I went off into the forests, where I joined up with a partisan group and survived until the liberation.

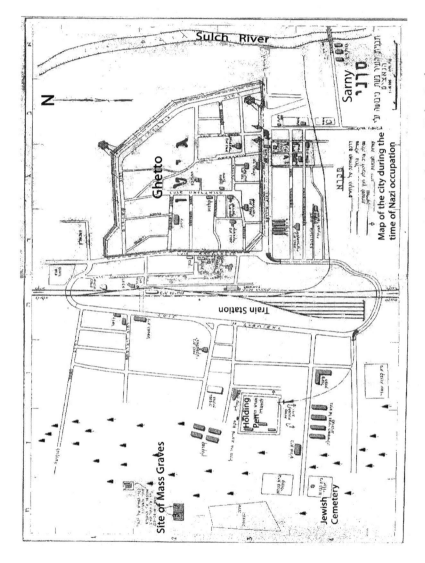

Map of Sarny during the time of the Ghetto 1941-42. Taken from the *Sarny Yizkor Book.*

41

Chapter Seven

The cellar had a bunker-style entrance, camouflaged and covered with leaves and debris. The entryway had double walls for protection, ensuring a tight compartment that was another safety feature. I blinked several times as my eyes adjusted to the darkness, finding about seven people huddled in this secret place, including Victor and his wife Dreizel, his younger brother Meyer, his father Jacob, and Victor and Dreizel's young son, Arnold. The space was about the size of a couch, which left little room for any of us. In fact, we could only sit, and our bathroom was one little board that opened up to the outside.

We heard the shooting on the first day. It was accompanied by the booms of grenades and the heart-shattering realization that this was the end for everyone we'd known in the ghetto. Arnold started crying, and his mother tried to quiet him down. I didn't really talk. I worried about my mother and what had happened to her. Later, I heard that the Germans had the Jews get undressed and killed them in mass graves.

The Nazis were still about, searching for any Jews hiding in the ghetto. That night, someone from our underground cell dared to poke a head out to observe what was going on. We discovered that those hiding in the attic of the house nearby had been discovered and dragged away.

We were cramped together for fourteen days, lacking food and water. All we had to eat were the remnants of pressed oil seeds that were normally fed to animals during winter months. As isolation, hunger, and the gravity of what had happened to my mother set in, I began crying myself to sleep without fail. I'd talk to her as if she was there, wishing and praying that she was still alive—even though my broken heart knew that couldn't be true. A pain developed in my stomach and chest from starvation, gnawing at me constantly. To this day, when I get hungry, the pain comes back and reminds me of hiding during the war.

When we couldn't take it anymore, we started to venture out to look for food. Eventually, I was spotted by a German soldier. He learned my routes and followed me one night, giving me a slip of paper with an address written on it. "This is my address," he said quietly. "Get there and see my mother. She will protect you until I come back." I figured he had romantic intentions and tore up the address as soon as he was out of sight. Thinking back, it could have been his way to save my life.

Things began to look desperate inside the cellar, and my Aunt Dreizel finally told me to go outside the ghetto and visit a Polish couple who lived near its border to beg for some food. "Tell them you are by yourself," she ordered me before sending me on my way.

Since the ghetto had been liquidated, and since we were near the edge of the ghetto as it was, I found my way to the Polish couple's house with little trouble. Their last name was Goldchevsky, and I knew them from before the ghetto liquidation. Mrs. Goldchevsky took me in and washed my hair with a bowl of water, caring for me as if I was her own child. She suddenly looked at me and said, "You know, we don't have any children. We are going to keep you behind the dresser, and, after the war, you will marry a Polish man."

When she said that, I went cold. I hadn't grown up like that, and even thinking about marrying someone outside the Jewish community was unheard of in my world. It was like she was sticking a knife in me, in my identity. But, I reasoned, it was silly to think about marriage when I needed to focus on surviving. *I'll do what I have to do*, I thought, and told her that, when I came back the following day to get some more food, I'd stay with her. She gave me some tomatoes and soup in a pail. I kept my aunt's advice in mind and didn't tell her about the others.

Despite my secrecy, it wasn't long before more people discovered where we were hiding. One day, a few young Ukrainians were searching for valuables hidden in people's backyards when they stumbled upon our hideout. I heard them whispering that they were going to call the police, and, right at that moment, I knew I had to leave. At the time, Dreizel and I were the only people inside. Victor had gone to the attic to hide because he was having a hard time breathing, and he eventually got caught with Dreizel. Arnold's grandfather made it out of the ghetto, along with Meyer. Arnold himself was given away to a Polish neighbor in Sarny across the street. After the war, his grandfather and uncle came to get him from the Polish family's house, but he started crying and didn't want to leave.[2]

Without any shoes on my feet, I began to run to the last place I'd been: the Golchevskys' house. When I arrived, they let me in, and Mrs. Golchevsky took watch by the window. I figured that the police would be looking for me, since they'd probably caught my cousins by now and knew how many people there were. Sure enough, I'd barely settled in when Mrs. Golchevsky yelled, "There are police, and they are coming to the back door!"

Breathless, I dashed out the front door and started to run again. In the chaos of my mind, I remembered the Ukrainian woman my mother had done alterations for all those months ago and headed toward her farm. Somehow, I made it. I pounded on her door a few times, but realized she wasn't home. Too tired to run anymore and too afraid to go back, I settled for hiding in the barn with her cows. It had to have been three or more hours before she finally arrived, not recognizing me at first. I'd gotten so skinny from not eating anything for days. When she finally realized who I was, she ushered me into the house and put a plate of food out for me. I was starving but found I couldn't eat.

"How is your mother?" she asked me.

"My mother is dead," I said quietly, picking at my food. "I've been in hiding."

---

2. For Arnold Frumin's account of the hideout and the events that followed, see: https://www.holocaustcenter.org/page.aspx?pid=806.

She encouraged me to eat, but I couldn't force the food down. "You can stay the night," she said finally, looking at me sadly. "But, in the morning, you must leave. My son belongs to the Nazi party, and I don't want him to find you here."

The next morning, she kissed me goodbye and advised me to head for a farm about two miles away. She also gave me a sack and a hatchet for digging potatoes, so I could tell anyone who questioned me that I was going out to dig potatoes in the village.

On my way to the farm, I ran into a group of Nazis who were blocking my path, practicing their shooting skills. There was no way to get around them, and I wasn't sure if I was bold enough to simply pass them by. It was then that I realized that I could not live as a hidden Jew. I needed to transform myself into a Polish woman and never cower before anyone. I strutted ahead, looking neither left nor right. Soldiers were at my elbow, but they did not notice me and kept on shooting.

By now, my feet were sore and blistered. The walk wasn't helping, as I had to trod amongst stiff corn stalks that had just been cut, which meant they were poking into my tender skin like thorns. I walked miles across fields and into the dark woods. It felt like a fairytale and a nightmare all at once. After what seemed like forever, I spotted a brick house in the middle of nowhere. When I finally knocked on the door I began sobbing, already blurting out my story to the Russian woman who answered. To my surprise, she greeted me immediately and supplied me with warm food. She was living alone and needed help, mainly with gathering wood for her stove. I set to work right away, picking up armfuls of wood with her help, telling her a little bit more about my situation.

We walked back to the house together to find a bicycle leaning against a tree, along with black boots and a black outfit.

"You have company," I told the woman, who followed my gaze.

Her eyes widened. "Quick—go and hide."

I crept into the house as silently as a mouse, looking for a good place to hide. There were several rooms with no furniture in them, but at last I came to a dark room with a small window and table with no tablecloth. I dove beneath the table as I heard a man's voice echo down the hall.

"The neighbors said there was a girl walking around here with some sort of tool for harvesting potatoes," he said. I could hear him making his way down the hall toward me. "Have you seen her?"

"I don't know," the Russian woman responded quietly. "I was in the city."

I heard the door to the room I was hidden in creak open, and a soldier walked inside. He was holding a bayonet and looked Ukrainian. Undoubtedly, he was looking for escaped Jews. Soldiers would catch them like flies and turn them in to the Nazis for a pound of salt. His eyes were fixated on the ceiling, looking for any fugitives hiding up in the attic. I could see the woman's feet behind him, and knew she could see me as well, because she moved to stand in front of me so her body blocked mine. My heart nearly stopped as the soldier paused, listening for any sounds or indication that I was there. My mind went through prayers over and over, desperately hoping I'd be spared. *Please, God, make him go away. If he doesn't see me, I'm going to survive the war.* As the minutes ticked by, my thoughts grew darker. *God, please, let him kill me with the gun and not the bayonet.*

I let out a breath as he started talking again. "How can you say you don't know if she's here? I saw her scarf and the harvesting tool in the kitchen. She must have been here."

The woman didn't reveal anything. If he caught me, she'd be in a lot of trouble—maybe even as much as me. "I was in the city," she repeated calmly. "Maybe she was here when I was gone."

"We're going to find her. I'll bring a hundred policemen here tomorrow and we'll search these entire woods." The soldier paced the room a couple more times, miraculously looking everywhere except where I was hiding. Finally, he eyed the open window. "These Jewish girls are so cunning and smart. She must've jumped out the window."

I shuddered as he ran out of the building, in pursuit of the phantom Jewish girl. After a few minutes, the Russian woman came in and hugged me tightly, kissing me and crying. "My child, I wanted to keep you here," she said, more tears streaming down her face, "but now I'm afraid."

I told her that she didn't have to tell me to go, because I knew it was time for me to move on again. Just as before, I set off without any shoes, running like a rabbit through the field.

Chapter Eight

I don't know how I was able to continue on, running and struggling through the fields in the darkness with no idea of where I was, but I managed to do so. Just as I slowed to take a rest, a light in the distance caught my eye. Walking toward it, I realized the light belonged to a little farmhouse. Although I knew it was risky to knock on the door of a total stranger, I was too tired to think of any other options.

A Polish woman answered and didn't ask any questions as she invited me into the house. She must have known I was Jewish, since no stranger walked around in the night like this—especially a teenaged girl. The woman lived with her two grown sons and a daughter who was around my age. One son appeared cognitively impaired, and the other son was not so swift either, but they all seemed to have sympathy for my situation.

The Polish woman finally invited me to stay with them until things cleared up, but I was hesitant to accept the offer. I'd heard that residents often turned in Jews who tried to find refuge in their homes, in exchange for a pound of salt from the police. The family seemed nice enough, but they were also poor. A pound of salt would be worth its weight in gold.

"I should just go," I said, finishing up the potatoes she'd given me.

"Are you crazy?" she asked me. "In the morning, when the sun comes up, they are going to catch you. You should stay here."

This will be my fate, I decided, nodding. I was too tired to go on any longer. If the family's intention was to turn me in, so be it.

She took me out to their barn to hide me from the police and offered me a place to sleep in the straw. I didn't hesitate to fall fast asleep, for once feeling safe among the straw and the cows next door. The next morning, the woman brought me a meal, sliding it through a slit in the door before shutting me in again. She would continue to do this three times a day for the next six months, providing me with little feasts of bread, sour milk, and maybe some mashed potatoes. I was also given a bucket to use as a bathroom.

While I'd found a place of refuge for the time being, nothing could stop my tears each night as mice scurried across the barn's rafters and winter set in quickly. I continued talking to my mother, holding on to the warm memories I had of her even as my hands grew numb and I shivered from the cold.

When it finally got too cold in the barn, the family allowed me to sleep in the house. The house itself was plain, with a dirt floor, but I would fall fast asleep right on top of the oven, wrapping myself up in an old curtain. I later found out that the Polish family's name was Yanacheck. They would often invite neighbors in, and I would hear the news they brought, usually about where the soldiers were capturing Jews. None of the neighbors knew I was there, but that didn't stop me from listening in on their conversations.

Police came through the area, so I was never completely safe. I had to spend the night in a schoolhouse attic one night, because the Yanachecks feared I'd be caught by the Nazis in the area who were searching houses. After the officers left, the family came back for me. It had been a long, frigid night. My fingers were so cold they had gone numb.

One day in the spring of 1943, the Ukrainians decided they wanted their own independent country. The Jews had been driven out, and now they wanted the Polish people killed as well. News spread that they were burning all the Polish farms in the region and killing their inhabitants with knives and hatchets. I didn't become aware of this until one morning, when I awoke to the sound of the Yanachecks packing in a hurry to leave their farm. When I asked what was going on, Mrs. Yanacheck tearfully explained everything.

"We're going to Germany," she finally said. "We're right along the border already—I think we can do it. You better come along too!"

We escaped in the middle of the night, rushing to the train station where we boarded a train headed for Krakow in occupied Poland. It would stop in Krakow for a time, then continue to Germany. To avoid raising suspicion, the Yanachecks told me to go by the name of Anna Kopera, a niece of theirs who had been recently killed. The real Anna had lived in a nice home with a big family, but the Ukrainians had come through their farm. After ordering the family to slaughter all their pigs to feed the soldiers, they'd hung them all.

The freight train afforded a barebones, uncomfortable ride. It ran on the rails for a while before making a stop in what looked like the middle of nowhere. I jumped off the car and ran into the grass, excited that I had a chance to stretch my legs and use the bathroom. But, as I turned back around to board the train again, I realized that it was already chugging away. I was left behind in the field, with no person in sight. Stranded, I began to cry. A thousand questions ran through my mind, unanswered in the silence that surrounded me. Where was I? Where should I go? I'd somehow survived the ghetto and evaded the police, but, after so many months of living in fear and anxiety, it was all crashing down on me.

I looked up from my hands to find a man walking down the train tracks. He had a lantern in his hand and his brow furrowed in concern as I continued sobbing.

"Little one, why are you crying so bitterly?" he asked as he approached. He was middle-aged and kind-looking, which consoled me a little. He must've been working on the train tracks and heard my cries.

I told him that I had been left behind and was separated from my family.

"Don't worry," he said. "I know there's another train coming soon, with large numbers of Russian prisoners of war. You can be reunited with your family when you get to Krakow."

I took his advice, and, sure enough, a train did arrive shortly after that. When I arrived at the station in Krakow, it didn't take me long to realize that I was completely alone—the Yanachecks had already taken the next train to Germany. But I didn't panic. I'd heard that Krakow had an office to interview people who wanted to work in Germany, which had a huge need for labor. I made my way over to the office and spoke to the office manager, explaining that I wanted to go to Germany to work. He frowned, crossing his arms across his chest.

"Why do you want to go to Germany? Don't you know they're starving there? There is no food!" He leaned in before I could answer, lowering his voice. "My sister-in-law has a large, untouched farm. She needs help desperately and would find room for you."

"Where is it?" I asked.

"A few kilometers from here. I can drive you there in the morning."

I agreed and slept on a park bench for the night. In the morning, the office manager came and picked me up. I was a little hesitant about going with him, not knowing if I could trust him or not. But, thankfully, he drove me directly to his sister-in-law's farm, a large place with a need for many more hands.

No one bothered to ask any questions, as, with my blonde hair and blue eyes, everyone thought I was Polish. I began working at the farm immediately in exchange for food and shelter. It was an unfair trade, because I worked for much more than what I received, but I was desperate enough to feel some sort of safety and consistency that I put up with it for a few months. I quickly learned how to milk the cows early in the morning and again late in the evening, along with watering the horses, cleaning the slop in the pig sty, and filling in time by picking weeds. Often, I'd find myself too tired to even eat dinner in the evenings, instead opting for a few extra hours of sleep.

There were many workers on the farm in the same condition as I was, but my lack of shoes gave me a huge disadvantage. After days of walking across rough pavement and stone, I developed a boil on the bottom of my foot that was filled with pus. I tried to deal with the pain, but eventually one of the farm's neighbors took pity on me and drained the boil with a needle. Unfortunately, the wound didn't have time to heal and the boil filled again, making the simplest tasks painful and tedious. Still, I tried the best I could.

We often worked in the fields pulling weeds together—the Polish workers and myself. They would speak about working in Germany, and, with the summer months coming up, I began to consider registering for work there, despite what the office manager had said about the food shortage. It turned out that I wouldn't have a choice, though, because, one day, I accidentally dropped my guard.

Everyone had continued to think I was Polish, a role that I played well thanks to the Yanachecks' education over the winter. I knew Polish and spoke it fairly well, and the family had taught me all their Christmas carols and religious beliefs while I'd lived with them. I also knew that they had confessions—something I'd never heard of as a Jew. Every year before Easter, the Polish Catholics would go to confess their sins to a priest.

Since it was around Eastertime, the conversation in the fields turned to church. A woman worker turned to me and asked if I'd gone to confession yet.

Somehow, in the fog of my exhausted brain and painful foot, I completely forgot everything I'd learned about confessions from the Yanachecks. "A confession? What is that?" I asked, instantly realizing my mistake as the woman paled and hastily withdrew.

I'd exposed myself as a Jew, and I needed to get out of the farm—*fast*.

The next day, I went to the woman who ran the farm and told her I wanted to go back to Sarny. She asked me if I was crazy, because there was no way for me to get across the border without any papers.

"I have my house," I lied, determined to make my getaway before word spread that I was a Jew in hiding. "And some distant family members."

She started pleading with me, saying that she needed me and telling me that the Germans took all the young people to work in factories. I wouldn't let myself be persuaded. I knew she wouldn't take me to the doctor for my foot, and the backbreaking labor I'd been doing for months now had taken a toll on me. The exhaustion and hunger never let up, and, now that I'd revealed my identity as a Jew, I knew it would only be a matter of time before I'd be hunted again. Finally, she angrily threw 10 zlotys at me and told me to go. I began the two-kilometer hike back toward the train station in Krakow.

My foot was throbbing by the time I reached my destination, and I knew that I wouldn't be able to go much farther. But then, a miracle happened. When I walked onto the platform, I caught sight of an old woman with a scarf, which held wooden shoes and material inside. It was as if the shoes had been waiting for me, as they were exactly my size, and the woman wanted 10 zlotys for them. I quickly paid her what I had. I truly believe my mother sent those shoes to me, to help me on my way.

Chapter Nine

I wasn't sure what I wanted to do in Krakow, only that I couldn't stay at the farm any longer and risk being exposed to the police. Soon after arriving at the station, I decided to try and go to the office that was seeking Polish volunteers to work in Germany.

The clerk in the office immediately began questioning me, asking me who my parents were and where I'd come from. I made up Polish names for my parents and told him I'd been born in Sarny. "My name is Anna Kopera," I finished convincingly, and thought I saw his eyes soften just a little.

"Anna Kopera." He mulled the name over. "Let me see your signed identification papers, then."

Of course, I didn't have any identification papers at all, much less for the Yanachecks' niece Anna Kopera. As I fumbled to come up with a response, the clerk waved his hand.

"If you do not already have the signed papers, you will not be accepted," he said, and my heart dropped a little. To my surprise, he frowned as he scanned the names on the volunteer list. "Ah, but Anna Kopera is already on our accepted list. What type of work do you prefer?"

I tried to contain my excitement, scarcely able to believe what he'd just asked me. The Yanachecks had saved me again. Instantly thinking of the hunger I'd constantly endured and the office manager's comment that Germany was undergoing a food shortage, I made sure to tell him that I wanted to work in a kitchen. I figured that, of all places, there'd definitely be food there, though I doubted I'd get a position in one. Beyond all expectations, I was placed to work in a resort reserved for German officers on leave from the fight. Most of them were wounded and were staying at the place—a hotel in the mountains—to recuperate from their injuries.

And so, I was officially Anna Kopera, a Polish worker on her way to Bavaria to work in the kitchens. I now bore the name of a dead woman who'd also been a victim of this gruesome war.

I was placed among the "Auslander" girls, non-German women who had been placed in the same position as me. We were held in a warehouse for three days while they gathered more girls who wanted to go work in Germany. When they had about 500 workers ready to leave, they told us all to get undressed so they could make sure we didn't have any diseases. My mind panicked as the girls around me began stripping off their clothes, and I realized I had no choice. I soon forgot I didn't have any clothes on as soldiers ushered us into a huge room, lining us up at different stations for examination. They looked at our heads for lice, and, despite not having a bath or washing up in weeks, my head was somehow clean. Other girls weren't so lucky. At one point, a soldier looked straight at me and patted me on the shoulder.

"Are you Ukrainian?"

"N—no," I stammered. "I'm Polish."

He looked me up and down, and I gritted my teeth. To him—to all the soldiers—the Auslanders weren't human. We were beneath them.

After I passed the examination, I joined the other chosen girls on the train headed toward Rottach in Bavaria, to a resort called Rottach-Tegernsee. As we stepped off the train and looked at our lavish surroundings, we gaped at the untouched luxury of the secluded hotel and restaurant. While most of the country was suffering, there was plenty of good food, liquor, and well-kept sleeping quarters here. I had found a place to eat like nowhere else during the Holocaust.

I was immediately assigned to menial tasks like cleaning the kitchen, doing dishes, and sweeping the floor—a welcomed relief from the conditions at the farm. From that moment on, I assumed Anna Kopera's identity totally. I went to church because the other girls went to church, I said prayers before bed, and I even wore a cross.

Soon after arriving, I found a new friend. Her name was Valla, and she was a Ukrainian girl from Russia. She was seventeen, just as I was at the time, and, since we were about the same size and she had a generous heart, she let me wear her clothes when mine started getting old and threadbare. Sometimes, she'd sneak goodies into her apron and give them to me, or we'd have a small picnic somewhere with her stolen goods.

Valla also helped me learn how to be Polish, even though she didn't realize it. I followed her example, which was easy to pick up on since we were bunkmates and became like sisters. We would talk in Russian together while I learned to speak German from everyone else. While I knew she wasn't anti-Semitic, I kept my identity a secret from her. I didn't want to slip up like I had at the farm, especially now that I had a good job with plenty of food.

Years later, when I moved back to Sarny and got married, I sent Valla a letter that explained my true identity. She wrote me back to say that she was so happy I'd survived, but she couldn't believe I was Jewish. She kept writing, "It's impossible!" I wrote her after that, when I was preparing to go to America, but I never got a response. I always wished I could have found her and brought her with me.

I was also on good terms with the main chef of the kitchens, a young German woman named Anna. She always saw to it that I was well-fed and kept me abreast of the latest news from the battlefront. I always wondered if she had a secret radio hidden somewhere, to know all these things. One day, she whispered in my ear, "Hitler is going to lose the war." She also told me when the Russians liberated Sarny, which gave me a faint glimpse of hope that the war would end, and soon.

Some of the girls weren't so friendly toward Jews, and once I nearly broke my cover because of a girl's comments. She said that the Germans were making soap out of the Jews. Although I wanted to slap her for saying such an awful thing, I kept quiet. Valla was beside me and kept silent as well. It just wasn't worth arguing with that girl, especially when my safety still hung in the balance. I hadn't forgotten what it felt like to run for my life, barefoot across fields and rocky ground.

In my two-and-a-half years working in Rottach—I arrived there in 1942 and left in 1944—I had very few awkward or otherwise bad encounters with my coworkers. There was a beautiful lake near the resort that I could see once in a while, though I was working most of the time. We got off at 2 p.m. on Wednesdays, which was my only off time. The people at the hotel were mostly kind to me. Anna and the waitresses always looked out for me, and one of the women working in the resort once helped relieve a boil that had formed on my neck.

I always tried to work hard, and was rewarded with a dress, shoes, and some nice things here and there throughout the time I spent there. I also tried my hand at snatching some bread from the kitchen now and then. One time, I'd stolen some bread and ran across a few emaciated Jewish men peeling mounds of potatoes in a basement. I couldn't bear it. I opened the door to the basement and threw in the bread I had. If I'd been caught, it would've cost me my life.

I wasn't the only one with sticky fingers. Valla's tendency to sneak little goodies for us was only the beginning. She eventually revealed to me that she had friends working in a Berlin factory who were hiding a Jewish girl. They wrote to her that they were hungry, and Valla would send the bread we'd pass by in the kitchen as often as she could. Once, she tried to steal some expensive roast beef for them. She might have gotten away with it, since she wrapped it up and addressed it to her friends, but, because she'd put a return address on the package, our supervisor found out about her crime. He slapped her hard across the face and she nearly lost consciousness, but she wasn't fired since the hotel needed all the help it could get.

Even so, Valla held a grudge against our supervisor after that, and we decided to leave in 1944. She had friends in Vienna, Austria, and wanted to go and find them. She'd also heard that foreigners were treated better in Vienna. With some persuasion, I agreed to go with her. We had little time to make preparations. Rumors had been circulating that the

Russians were approaching with little to nothing to stop them, and our supervisors and other workers had already begun to disappear. Although Valla tried to find our papers, which the supervisor kept somewhere in his office, she had no luck, and we were forced to leave without them. I bought two colorful straw hats—a common summer style back then—to help us disguise ourselves. When we put them on, we looked like two young German girls.

We left on a Wednesday, the only day we got off, at 2 p.m., and headed to the train station. Of course, when we boarded the train, we found inspectors walking through the aisles checking everyone's identification papers. "*Ausweis*, Ausweis" they said to each person, who promptly handed over their documents and tickets. I nudged Valla with my elbow and hissed at her to turn toward the window. As we did, the inspectors passed right by us. Apparently, they weren't concerned about the two innocent, young German women looking outside.

Chapter Ten

When we arrived in Vienna, we were greeted by turmoil. The city was undergoing liberation, and there were soldiers everywhere. Valla and I hurried to the employment office, where I explained we were looking for work. Since it had been hard for Valla to pick up the German language, I did most of the talking. German had plenty of similarities to Yiddish, so I'd picked it up quickly—though I had to be careful not to accidentally start speaking Yiddish when speaking German. To avoid this, and to make sure my words would sound as natural as possible, I always silently rehearsed what I was about to say in German before actually speaking.

The clerk at the office looked at us and asked us where we'd come from. I knew that Berlin had been bombed, so I rattled off a story about having to leave from there to look for work elsewhere.

"All the way from Berlin?" she asked me, unconvinced.

"We just took the first train we saw." I didn't know what to say—what did I know? The train had been going to Vienna, and here we were. It was as simple as that.

After a few moments, the clerk shrugged. "Where were you working in Berlin?"

"A restaurant in a hotel," I answered truthfully.

We were assigned to a fancy hotel in Vienna, but had hardly settled in, when we first heard the sirens. People who'd fled from Munich to the resort in Bavaria had told us about the bombs. But when I heard—and *felt*—the sounds of sirens and panic, I began to understand what those people had gone through.

We fell in step with a group from the hotel and were scrambling toward a shelter when the first bomb hit the ground, rattling through my bones. Almost instantly, I felt like I was choking. Little did I know it was the fumes from the bomb. Before I knew it, I'd passed out. Everything went black and all the sounds faded away. It wasn't until I woke up on a stretcher in the basement that I realized what had happened.

Soon, we learned the routine of things. Valla and I would clean and do dishes, and everyone would head to the shelter at around 11 a.m. each day, when the British and Americans rained bombs on the city. It was frightening, sitting huddled in the basement as people died and fought above us. On my third day in Vienna, the bombs were especially close. We heard one go off very close to our temporary housing, and one of the waiters opened the door to the basement to see where it had landed. I peeked out from behind him, curious myself, but, the second he opened the door, he crumpled to the ground. A blast had hit him fatally.

After that, Valla and I went back to the employment office, troubled and frightened from our run-in with the bombs. The clerk took pity on us and assigned us outside the city, 40 kilometers from Vienna and well away from the fighting. They sent us to a camp in the middle of nowhere where they trained sixteen- to eighteen-year-old boys to fight on the front lines. When we arrived, they had about two dozen officers. We worked in the kitchen there, and, although it wasn't quite the life we were used to at the restaurants, we both agreed that it was better than living with bombs raining down on us each day.

It wasn't long before the Russians came to the little town, bringing the battle with them. We sprinted into a nearby field and laid down amid gunfire and shouts, sure that this was it—this was the end of the world. But, by the end of the evening, we were ordered to get on trucks and were transported back into Vienna. The city was in shambles, and soldiers' bodies and horses were strewn everywhere, even on the streets. A fight broke out right there when a German sniper started shooting at us and the Russian soldiers, who returned gunfire. We ran across the street, where a Russian soldier had taken out a big window of a storefront with his rifle.

"The shop is open," he said in Russian, keeping his gun at shoulder level. "Take what you want."

I was shaking so badly that I could hardly comprehend his words, but I scrambled inside the shop with the others and began looking for shoes. Despite the great number of shoeboxes strewn everywhere, only one box had a shoe—a single shoe—in it. Nevertheless, I gathered up a coat and a few dresses, trembling at the thought of stealing these from a store even though we were in the middle of a war zone. One of the Russian soldiers laid out a sheet for me, putting the items in the middle of it and tying it up in a bundle so I could carry it more easily.

We slowly made our way out the front door, following a few soldiers. I heard a buzzing sound coming my way, like a big bee or insect flying past. Almost instantly, the Russian soldier in front of me fell to the ground, hit with a bullet in the ankle. "*Noga, noga!*" he cried, clutching the wound. "My leg!"

When Valla and I found an abandoned home to take shelter in for the night, I took off my blue summer coat and noticed a tear in its lining. Inspecting it more closely, I realized that a bullet had passed through both the coat and its lining. It had gone right through the left side, next to my heart. A couple more inches, and I would've been killed. To this day, this miracle reminds me why I believe in God.

Because Valla had family to go back to, she eventually went home. I didn't have anybody, and my identity was still a secret, so I knew I'd have to find somewhere else to work. Following the advice of a Russian solider, I made my way to a field hospital in the middle of the chaos. They hired me right away, since I knew the language and was willing to work in any capacity. The hospital was a large operation, with about six thousand people either being treated or working to treat wounded soldiers. I spent my days doing menial tasks—cleaning urinals, helping patients out of bed, and acting as a nurse's aide—as the war waged on, coming closer and closer to an end.

Around this time, I discovered a Russian soldier who spoke in a way that was different from the rest. I recognized the Jewish accent immediately, and sought him out, hoping to confide in him. But when I confronted him about his Jewish heritage, he shook his head and denied it.

"Don't worry about what nationality a person is," he told me. "Worry about whether or not a man has a good character."

Sobered, I left him alone. It still wasn't a good time to be a Jew, and I knew my identity would have to stay a secret.

It was only a matter of time before the clinic decided to move out of chaotic Austria to the border of Hungary. It was there that we were liberated in May of 1945.

On the day of liberation, everyone went to the square downtown in Sopron, Hungary and started dancing and celebrating. I couldn't find it within myself to rejoice. Instead, I was so hurt and bitter that everyone else was so happy that all I could do was stand in the corner and cry. How many Jewish lives could have been spared in Hungary and Romania had they had a little compassion? That was the question I kept asking myself, watching as everyone danced and forgot about the annihilation of the Jews. How could they simply forget about the suffering we'd gone through?

I began to think I didn't even want to be Jewish anymore, but, in that same moment, I realized that God had spared my life for a reason. I had to stay a Jew. Most of my people had been killed or driven out, and there were already plenty of Gentiles. I had to represent the voices of all who had passed on—my father, my mother, my brother, my friends and family. If I gave up being Jewish, none of it would mean anything.

From that day forward, I never questioned being a Jew again.

Chapter Eleven

As I continued working at the hospital as the Polish girl Anna Ko-pera, I finally settled into a comfortable routine. I slept in the *op-shi-shietze*, a big cabin where all the women lived when they weren't working. Since Valla had left, I found new friends from Ukraine who would always say *zablotskhah* to me, because I was from the same vicinity as they were. They treated me like family and were always quiet and polite. Once, we went to a show together and came back a little too late—maybe by ten or twenty minutes. We were stopped by the police and they put us in jail, even though I complained to the guard that we didn't do anything wrong. Since we had forgotten our papers in the cabin, the guard informed me that we'd be spending the night in jail until he could verify that we did, indeed, work for the hospital. He also gave me a key to his room, which made me fearful that he wanted to do something to me—so I quieted down and slept in the cell overnight. The next morning, he verified that we worked for the hospital and let us go.

After a couple months in Sopron, the hospital moved to Budapest. There, despite all the times I'd faced death in the past, I nearly met my downfall. Fruit was almost absent in Budapest, so, when I saw a peasant woman hawking bags of cherries, my mouth watered. I approached the woman to buy some, but I had no money. By trading some of my precious bits of bread, I convinced her to give me her cherries. Although I worked in a hospital, I didn't even think to wash the cherries before eating them. I found out they were contaminated soon enough. I became very ill and had to spend two agonizing weeks fighting to stay alive. My stomach ached all the time, and I was continually bleeding—so much so that they put me in a separate area of the hospital. Instead of nursing the patients, I became one myself. When I recovered, the hospital supervisor informed me that they were moving to the Russian-occupied city of Galatz, Romania. We'd been in Hungary only three months.

Although life was relatively normal in Romania, it held a number of unexpected surprises. For the first time since my childhood, I began to see more Jewish people out in the open. I made friends with a Jewish mother and daughter who were working at the hospital. The mother explained that they had survived the war working for the Russians and asked me why I had such a pink complexion compared to her daughter, who was darker. It was nice to have other survivors working alongside of me in the hospital, especially since I'd felt alone for so long as a secret Jew.

Another instance occurred over a pair of boots. I'd nearly walked holes through my old shoes, and decided I needed a new pair. I was recommended to a little shoe shop, where I instantly noticed the shoemaker and his family were Jewish. As I waited, they confirmed my suspicions by speaking Yiddish to each other.

"I hope you aren't going to say anything about me," I said in Russian, giving them a smile. "I can understand every word you're saying."

They froze, staring at me and narrowing their eyes a little. "How?" they asked.

"I'm Jewish." A shiver crept up my spine as I realized that this was the first time I'd said outright that I was Jewish since my childhood.

They didn't believe me, mainly because I didn't look the part. They began to speak to me in Yiddish, and I realized that I couldn't even utter a word in reply. So many years of using Russian, Polish, and German had erased my memories of Yiddish.

"She must have worked for a Jewish family and picked up a few words," the shoemaker's helper, a young man, said in Yiddish.

The shoemaker nodded. "There isn't any way she's Jewish."

He strode over to the window and picked up a Romanian paper, handing it to me and pointing out a block of text in Hebrew.

"I can read that," I said, and read the entire thing in Hebrew. I hadn't spoken it in so long, yet I remembered every word and pronunciation.

"You *are* blood!" They started kissing me and hugging me, already talking about how they were going to help me find a *choisen*, a groom, that evening.

True to their word, they took me to another shoemaker's place that night and introduced me. I tried to be polite, but I knew this match would never work—and getting married was the farthest thing from my plans. Not to mention, in Poland, marrying a shoemaker was considered a very bad match...the worst! Still, I got a good deal on my boots.

The shoemaker's family also later took me to a synagogue, which was full of Jewish people, both children and the elderly. The moment I stepped foot into the building, tears filled my eyes. It was as if nothing had happened in this town. They carried Torahs and sat just as they had in the synagogue back home. My heart broke a little at the memories flooding my mind, of all the times I'd sat with my mother upstairs as my father and brother took their seats downstairs. My whole family was gone, and it hurt—more than I could ever describe.

When I asked how all these people had survived, they told me that the mayor of the town hadn't given away the Jews.

Chapter Twelve

Three months after we'd arrived in Romania, the hospital announced that it would be returning to Russia. Without ceremony, all employees were presented with train tickets. We could travel along with the medical team to Russia, remain in Romania, or return to our hometowns. I opted to return to Poland and seek any remaining relatives, friends, or neighbors. I had a feeling that no one would be left in my hometown, David-Horodok, since the soldiers hadn't taken any Jews to work—they'd simply murdered them all. Still, I hoped that, if I headed that way, I'd eventually run into someone I knew.

Strangely enough, the train stopped in Sarny and wouldn't keep going. I waited with the other passengers for hours and hours, but the conductor had no answer for us. He kept saying, "Just wait—repairs are being made."

Eventually, I lost patience. Although it would be quite a hike on foot, I decided to chance it. It did start to rain, but, luckily, I had a raincoat this time.

Sarny turned out to be the better destination anyway, since most of the Jews in the area had resettled there. I had high hopes when I marched into town, after seeing all the Jews who had survived in Romania. Sarny had been a second home to me in the past, with friends and family all around.

Sadly, I could not find anyone I personally knew. There were friendly Jews all around the city who greeted me, and they provided me with some food. That night, I found my way back to the Frumins' old house in the ghetto—the only place I remembered how to get to. I found out that little Arnold's parents hadn't made it, but his grandfather, aunt, and uncle—Meyer, Victor's brother—had survived. They were living in the old house for the time being, while they worked to collect Arnold from the Christian family he'd been given to after they'd all been caught.

Since Arnold had been given to the family when he was just five years old, the Frumins would have a hard time convincing him to leave. Prying him away from the only world he could remember would be a tearful event. Meyer was in his twenties now, and he invited me in right away. I slept on a mattress and bed made up of two large boards nailed together. That suited me just fine. I was too tired and disappointed to think of luxury bedding.

On the other hand, I had reached a place of safety. I no longer felt like Anna Kopera, the Polish girl who worked in the kitchens or at the hospital. Perhaps I was Basia again, the Jew. But what did that mean? I was all alone, with no idea of what my future would entail.

In the morning, a butcher came by the house to deliver some meat. Within a few hours of his departure, another knock sounded at the door. It was none other than Harold (Hershel-Tzvi) Perlstein, my third cousin who I'd known from the ghetto. The butcher had described me to him and told him I was staying in the Frumins' old house, and he'd wanted to come as soon as possible to see if it was really me. I was shocked that he'd found me, and he was surprised that I had made it out of the ghetto all those years ago.

"How is your wife? Your child?" I asked, remembering that he had been married and had a little girl as well.

"They did not survive," he responded. "I fought with the Russian partisans, and now I am alone."

We spoke a little while longer, and it became obvious that he was interested in me. He left me with a few parting words: "I'll be coming over to see you tomorrow."

He did just that the next day, and the day after. In the meantime, his sister and other relatives spoke to me of his attributes. This led me to believe a marriage proposal was on its way.

I didn't have much of a mind for marriage, and there was a large age gap between Harold and me. I was twenty, and he was thirty-two, albeit a good-looking thirty-two. On the other hand, I didn't know where to go from here. I had nothing—no possessions, no money, no place to live, and no relatives or friends to help or advise me. I was young, naïve, and clueless as to what marriage entailed, but I didn't really have another choice. If I was going to survive, I'd just have to find a way to adjust to the thought of marrying Harold.

That's what I did when Harold proposed to me and arranged an immediate marriage. Five days after I'd met him, in December of 1945, we were married. It was a small *chuppah* wedding, and no one stood for me. The only people there were Harold's sister Chaika, her children, and a friend who performed the ceremony. At the time, it wasn't a marriage of love; it was a marriage of survival. I thought that, if he would be nice to me, I would fall in love.

I moved into Harold's home with a new name, Basia Perlstein. Within two months, I was pregnant with my first child.

The times were very abnormal then, with the whole Polish and German economy upside down. Most transactions, for food or otherwise, were made with bartering on the black market. Harold had hidden away some pre-war dollars and recovered them. He had ended up in jail before for exchanging Russian rubles for this gold, and, when we got married, he had 250,000 rubles in the closet. With his business acumen, he also took advantage of the cigarette shortage and built a large undercover operation. He actually arranged to have three loads of cigarettes imported and distributed.

I myself was drawn into his effort in a big way. I'd hide large amounts of illegal cigarettes under my clothing so we could make a profit, and Harold would turn our efforts into gold. Eventually, though, I tired of this life. I wanted to go to Israel like his sister had months before and didn't want Harold to end up in jail again for his illegal cigarette business. Harold, though, wanted to go to America. He had a cousin there and was convinced that we could always go to Israel if we didn't like America. After months of talking back and forth, I finally agreed with his plan.

It took a few more months for Harold to finally agree to give up his lucrative business, after I gave him an ultimatum: Either I was going to Israel alone, or the both of us were going to America. After the war had ended in 1945, Jewish survivors in Russian-occupied Poland were clamoring to escape communism and leave the country. Pogroms and anti-Jewish atrocities were raging over the entire area, and I didn't want my unborn child to have to grow up in this environment.

As awful as these riots were, they brought about an unexpected advantage: monthly transports to D.P. (displaced persons) camps in Bavaria, southern Germany. The camps were in American-occupied Germany, which meant we'd be safer and one step closer to getting to America. Most of our friends and acquaintances had already taken the trip to a D.P. camp, and I was anxious to get out of Sarny while we still could.

A surprise incident lent further inspiration for me to rush departure. I saw a gypsy woman wearing billowing skirts wandering nearby. She stopped me and told me that she was hungry. "Give me a slice of bread. I'll tell you your fortune in exchange," she said. Intrigued, I agreed to the idea. Despite the bread shortage, we had plenty, thanks to Harold's business. She sat me down, opened my hand, and ran her fingers across my palm.

"You have lost your loved ones," she said. "You now are alone. You will not remain here for long but will go on a long journey over a large body of water. You will give birth to three children."

It all came true. I was already pregnant, to start off. Now, Harold had to make his move. In order to get a transport to the D.P. camp in Germany, we'd have to get out of Russian-occupied Sarny and cross the Russian border without getting caught. A friend of Harold's was forming a small group to do just that. We signed up with money, sealing the deal. All in all, seven of us walked together. We were to reach our goal on foot, climbing the Alps. It would be difficult, but we had to try.

Chapter Thirteen

Climbing mountains was difficult enough but going undetected across the guarded borders was another matter. We had to cross into Czechoslovakia, then Austria, and from there we entered Germany. We bribed the guards at the border obstructions and often walked under the cover of darkness, holding on to each other so we didn't get lost. It was a long, treacherous journey. We arrived in the summer of 1946.

The D.P. camp was in Bad Reichenhall, in the heart of Bavaria. It had been a large German soldiers' barrack, but, since the Americans had taken control, it housed approximately six thousand Jews. Upon registration, they asked us our desired destination. I stated "Palestine," while Harold expressed his desire for America—where we would eventually end up. We lived in brick buildings with good-sized apartments, and the Jewish Joint Distribution Committee had been given the right to administer all the camp functions. UNRA of the United Nations was also active, and Jewish survivors themselves provided policing duties while American military police (MPs) were only brought in for emergencies.

Even though I was pregnant, I didn't hesitate to join the in-house workers. Being fluent in Yiddish, Hebrew, Polish, Russian, and some German, I assumed the position of secretary, a *mascarah*, of the large Betar faction. I would write minutes for our meetings and give reports in Hebrew. There were other groups where survivors joined and lived together, such as Zionist, religious, and hometown clubs. Harold grew busy, as well. He helped distribute food provided by the JDC and UNRA, and care packages from the United States. It all passed through his hands. He made some money from his efforts, because he would sell the food and was also still smuggling cigarettes.

To keep the people hopeful and reduce anxiety, the camp organized many programs and dinners. They even had ballroom dancing sometimes, and little parties to raise people's spirits. But everyone was on edge, waiting for their future to unfold. Would they be allowed to enter the United States? And if so, when?

It didn't help that developments at the camp were slow. Those with relatives in the States topped the entry lists, and they had to go through an approval process since the government had to be sure that the newcomers would be adequately housed and fed in America. There were also a number of pregnancies that had emerged after the Holocaust. Women wanted to be sure that the wartime atrocities had not destroyed their fertility.

I had our first child on October 25, 1946, in the compound's makeshift hospital. Despite not knowing anything about childbirth, and despite being in a hospital, I gave birth by myself in a tiny room. By the time I started screaming, the baby was already on her way. I held her in my lap until a doctor and nurse came in and cut the cord. Harold and I had made a deal: If the baby was a girl, we would name her Debra (Dvora) after his mother, and if it was a boy, we would name him after my father. So, Debra it was.

I had to stay in the hospital for ten days after giving birth, because Debra nearly died from malnutrition. My breastmilk was off-color and not up to standard for my little daughter's growth, and she lost weight quickly. Since we didn't have powdered milk available, I was helpless. I didn't know how I could save my baby. Thankfully, the doctor at the camp made an excellent suggestion. He told me to boil some rice, strain it, and use the residue as a substitute for milk. Within a few days, Debra began picking up strength. I also started to feed her farina in tiny amounts. Her next step was eating table food. From birth on, Debra's beauty shone far above most babies' born in the camp. Those passing by would gape at her as I walked with her in the carriage.

We had planned to leave the D.P. camp in 1947, after we received an exit visa from Harold's cousin in America, but our plans were delayed when we signed as witnesses to a young Russian-Jewish couple, who falsely claimed that they were survivors of the Holocaust. Because our names were on their paperwork, we were moved to the bottom of the list. I wanted to go to Israel rather than endure the long wait, but we ended up staying in the camp for three years, from 1946 to 1949. By the time we left for America, Debra was almost three years old.

Finally, on May 18, 1949, we got to the northern seaport at Bremerhaven and boarded a small army ship called *The Marine Jumper*. I was twenty-four years old, Harold was thirty-five, and Debra was two-and-a-half. The ship was overcrowded with eager survivors, most of whom had never seen saltwater, let alone boarded a ship heading into the Atlantic Ocean. As a result, almost everyone suffered a bout of seasickness. It was no wonder, with waves angrily attacking the ship, rocking it back and forth as water splashed on board. Harold, myself, and Debra had no trouble, but the long journey seemed as if it would never end. We slept in bunk beds, and I met a woman who was going to Chicago. At the end of ten days, we finally arrived in New York.

My first memory of America was the great Statue of Liberty, welcoming us from land. Seeing that monument made my heart light, and I was grateful we'd all survived the long voyage. When we got off the boat, we shuffled through customs, and two women from the Joint Distribution Committee came to greet us. They brought us to a restaurant to eat and clean up, letting us take time to look around. We were transfixed by the sight of so many New Yorkers walking the streets, along with the many buildings and busy city life. Harold pointed out all the cars. He was so excited to one day buy a car.

"We'll take you to the train to go to Detroit," one of the women said, in Yiddish, because I couldn't speak any English. "You'll see how people live there. Everyone has seven rooms!"

We were going to Detroit because both my husband and I had family that had settled there before the war. I had two aunts on my mother's side who lived there, Chana and Pesel. My mother's brother, Abraham, had also taken residence in America, but had died in a car accident in the 1920s. My father's sister, Rifka, lived in Detroit with her husband, Morris Dobrowitsky. Harold had a cousin, Harold Sher, who had lived in America for a while, too.

Everyone was there when we arrived at the station. It was a fine reception, and my aunt Rifka offered her home for us, so we could spend a few days and nights resting. I had never met my Aunt Rifka. She was my father's older sister, and she and I were the only two left from my father's family. She'd married her husband, Mottel (Morris) Rosenblum, in David-Horodok and had a daughter Tiebel in 1912. Morris had soon departed for America and then sent for his wife and daughter, who'd had to wait until after War World I ended before they could make the voyage. They'd arrived in 1922, before I was even born. They'd left behind the house in David-Horodok that my father and his brother Shevach had split as a duplex and raised their families in.

Rifka had been in touch with us through letters we'd received at the D.P. camp. She had already been in America for almost thirty years when I met her at the train station, and had two more children, Max and Ida. She and Morris had done well with a stockyard and lots of property on Chicago Boulevard in Detroit.

Unfortunately, we did not get off to a good start, perhaps due to my naiveté about how things in America worked. We got into a heated argument over renting an apartment from her. She might have kept us longer, if I'd thought to ask her how much she wanted for rent. We regrettably developed a falling out within the short time we were with her—probably one week. I believe she probably assumed I was going to move in and freeload off her for years. We then turned to Harold's cousin, Harold Sher, for assistance until we got on our feet.

I began to understand what the Joint Distribution woman had been talking about, when she'd said everyone in Detroit had seven rooms. Most people here didn't live in apartments; they lived in houses. It wasn't long before my mother's uncle (my grandmother's brother), Michael Taich, got in touch with me. He was renting a house in Detroit and invited us to come live with him for twenty-five dollars a month—fifty percent of the total rent. He was well-known in Zionist circles in Detroit and was a very nice man. We lived happily with him and his wife Golda for a time, occasionally hearing about their three children who lived in Texas.

My husband's cousin and my Aunt Rifka had paid for our passage, and Harold began working right away to pay them back. He accepted a job offer from his cousin Harold Sher, who owned a local bar at an eastside location. After a short period of doing simple tasks, Harold understood the business. He became a bartender, and, after six or seven months, Mr. Sher presented Harold with the idea of becoming a full partner. Harold was eager to accept. I objected, because I knew Mr. Sher just wanted to semi-retire and take it easy while Harold did all the work. "You know the business, we have the money," I urged him. "Let's look around for our own bar."

The partnership deal went on hold, and we not only bought one bar, but also another one for me to operate. It turned out that I had a nose for good opportunities in business, and I got quite aggressive in understanding the market.

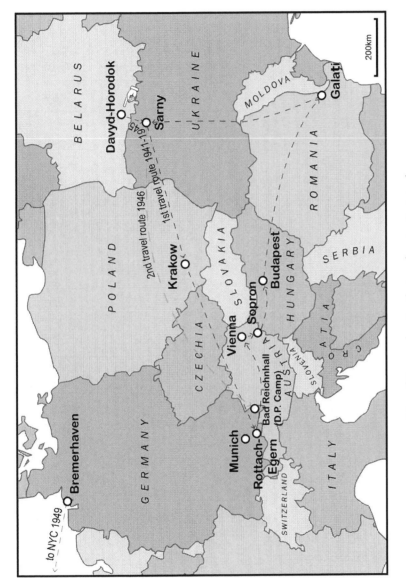

Map of Europe showing the travel routes Basia took.

75

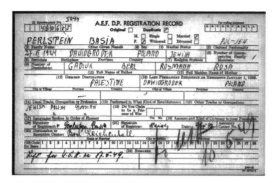

The D.P. camp registration ID card for Basia Perlstein and her stated intention of immigrating to Palestine.

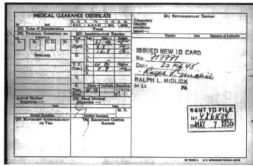

The back of Basia's D.P. camp ID card.

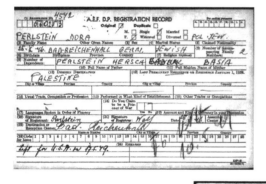

The D.P. camp registration ID card for the daughter of Basia and Hersch: Dora (Debra) Perlstein.

The D.P. camp registration ID card for Hersch Perlstein. Note his desired destination is listed as the United States.

Nominal roll call of the D.P. Camp at Bad Reichenhall on August 1, 1947. The front page of the report is accompanied with the page listing Hersch, Basia, and Dora Perlstein.

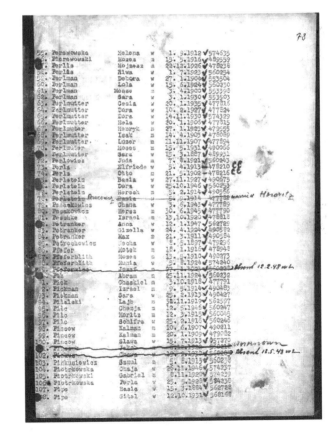

A. E. F. ASSEMBLY CENTER REGISTRATION CARD

D.P. Assembly Center roll call card for Basia Perlstein.

A list in Polish from the D.P. Camp, which details the registrant's year of birth, parents' names, and last known address in 1939. Basia Perlstein lists her parents' names as Berko and Drying (Dreizel or Reizel) and the Polish spelling of her hometown: Dawidgrodeak. Her address in the D.P. Camp was "Korfantego 25."

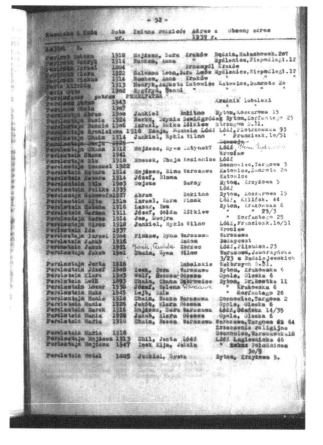

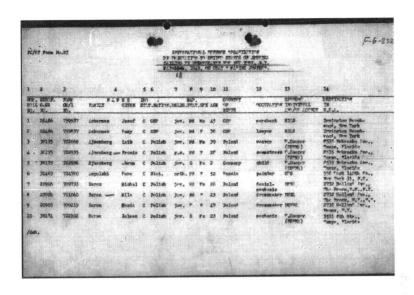

The ship manifest from May 18, 1949 of the *Marine Jumper*, which left Bremerhaven, Germany for New York. Hersch (35), Basia (24), and Dora (2) Perlstein are listed with their intended destination of Bea's Aunt Rifka's house on Chicago Boulevard in Detroit, Michigan.

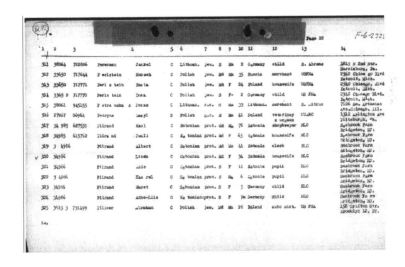

Chapter Fourteen

M y part in the new deal required a radical adjustment to my early
months in Detroit. Our bars needed a fairly constant presence to
watch over them, and I still had to raise my little daughter, Debra. With
my limited English, and being a young woman in my twenties, I wasn't
sure how I'd be able to handle a drinking crowd and all that entailed. But,
somehow, I managed, and even became a back-up bartender. To take care
of Debra, I hired a maid of sorts to cover the time when I was gone. Besides doling out hard drinks, I helped manage the entire business without
revealing who I was to the crowd of patrons.

There was no entry fee to the bar or the floor show that followed. We
offered chicken wings and similar food bites for only thirty-five cents but
made it all up and more by selling different whiskies. Middle-class couples
were our basic patrons, so we had little trouble. However, we did have a
bouncer to keep things in order. There were moments when I could enjoy
the floor show—a comedian, singer, or small bands—but what was most
pleasant was the sound of money that gushed into my bar, and Harold's
as well.

In the meantime, we purchased a house in Detroit. It was a brick,
two-story house on Savory Street, and cost us $13,000. Later, we would
find a little house in Oak Park, and finally a top-notch place in Southfield.
We needed a car early on, since both Harold and I needed to drive to
work and back. I pulled out three hundred dollars I'd stashed away and

told Harold to seek a good used car as a start. Instead, he returned with a brand-new Chevrolet. The success at the bars bolstered Harold's ego, and he began smoking cigars, dressing better, and sporting his new car. Eventually, we both piloted Cadillacs only.

During this time, I registered for night school, determined to get my citizenship papers. Although many survivors and other foreigners started with me at night school, most did not stay for long. Very few completed the full three-year course. By the time I had finished, I could read and write English fairly well. My English speaking improved quite a bit, but I retained my old-world accent. I gained my citizenship papers.

On October 31, 1950, I gave birth to my second daughter, Rita. Harold was hoping for a boy. When the doctor called him and said, "Trick or Treat, Mr. Perlstein—you have a lovely daughter," Harold hung up on him. Despite this, Harold and Rita grew to be very close. In June of 1954, I gave birth to my third daughter, Bonnie. We later moved to a home in Oak Park where we raised our three daughters, who were a joy.

Business still continued as usual, and, at our peak, we had three bars—the Eagle Bar, the 12th Street Bar, and the Hobby Bar. As the bars thrived, I grew worldly with them. Now, I could banter with women and men alike—whether at the tables or the bar. I could even use English slang, despite my heavy accent. It was hard work, extending over long hours, yet it was an exciting time and very rewarding monetarily.

Of course, the bar business had its issues, as well. In all my years during the Holocaust keeping ahead of the Nazis in Poland, Germany, Hungary, and Romania, I had been successful in fending off all sleazy advances or propositions from men. But even Detroit had its share of difficulties, especially since I was still younger than thirty and was commonly out and about in the late evening hours. One such incident occurred when I got a flat tire on my regular drive to the bar. I was stranded on the side of the road, waving toward passing cars with no results, when someone finally stopped. Two young men parked nearby and volunteered to help. They quickly hopped out of their vehicle and changed the tire.

Grateful as I was, I had no cash in my purse. However, I wanted to do a little more than thank them. So, I offered to lead them to the bar, where

I would be able to provide them with some drinks. The two guys readily accepted and trailed me there, and I settled back into my bartender's post. I assumed they would leave the bar after they were finished, but instead they hung around. After a couple hours and plenty of extra drinks, other customers started coming in for the evening and I escaped into the back room.

Then, there was the situation with a police officer. One night, I was caught speeding on the highway, and a hefty officer in his forties or older pulled me over. I thought I was going to get a speeding ticket, but instead the officer ogled me and said, "You know, I can avoid giving you a ticket, but you will have to come along with me." Knowing full well what his intentions were, I strung him along. He eventually revealed that he had a wife and children, but I held a special appeal to him. Thinking fast, I pleaded with him to let me get to work on the promise I would meet him the next morning at my address. I did give him an address, but it was a false one. I never saw him again, and he never gave me a ticket.

In 1965, one of the scariest situations at the bar occurred. I was working the counter in the Eagle Bar one evening when a man walked in and held a gun up to me, demanding all my money. He shot me before making off with the cash, and I had to be rushed to Henry Ford Hospital. There, I lost a kidney. This awful incident seemed to foretell the 1967 race riots, which changed our profitable ventures rapidly. We suffered severe damage to the bars, and it was apparent that it no longer was safe to remain or relocate. Without too much hesitation, we unloaded the bars for whatever we could get. Fortunately, we had made and saved enough money for Harold and me to have time to look for another opportunity.

We found an unlikely field to get involved in: nursing homes. We had become friendly with the Rosenzweig family, and Felix Rosenzweig was the owner of a nursing home. He started to take Harold to the meetings of the nursing home group. At the meetings, they discussed all current developments in the business. The need for nursing homes was great, which intrigued Harold and me tremendously. Despite the demand for nursing homes, there weren't any homes for sale—but we were determined to break into the business. We decided to buy a plot of land in Taylor Township and build a home from scratch. It was an expensive mistake, because we never even got the home built. Government restrictions for nursing homes and zoning problems forced us to give up and sell the land.

We didn't stop there and continued looking for places to establish our nursing home. Our break came when Harold heard that an elderly Irish couple was looking to retire and sell their two homes. I researched the properties with Harold and concluded that the homes were fully occupied and operating smoothly. I urged him to make an offer for the two homes on the east side of Detroit. Harold, however, wanted to consult with Mr. Rosenzweig first. Felix seized the chance to join us in our efforts to get the home. I did not like the partnership idea, and, when Felix claimed he had a cold and didn't appear at a showdown meeting with the couple, I pressed Harold for us to go at it alone.

At long last, we agreed to the terms with the couple. We were now the proprietors of the nursing homes. As we'd done with the bars, Harold and I split up responsibilities between the two homes. Mine was not as large and roomy as the other one, but it had all its beds fully occupied. My regular hours were 8 a.m. to 5 p.m., but both Harold and I were on call at all hours. The nursing homes also had nurses, nurse's aides, and doctors who always had to be present. Inspectors from the state capital in Lansing frequently called to check up on our facilities, and we became known for providing good food and proper facilities. A clean health report followed each inspector's visit.

Every morning, I would make rounds to check on every patient, in addition to the nurse's visits. I wanted to keep everything in order. I also collected the rents and oversaw all the employees. I witnessed the home transition from mostly women occupying the beds to mostly new arrivals from the military. Many of these military folks were shell-shocked and required specific care. Whenever Harold needed my help, I went over to the larger facility to help him manage it.

Within a few months, we moved like a well-oiled machine. We operated in joint harmony and even lunched together in a nearby restaurant. Our new wealth streamed in, which allowed us to get involved with the Jewish community and its concerns. Our philanthropy in particular raised money for causes related to Israel. A highlight of this was being invited to greet Menachem Begin at a hotel in New York City. Locally, we joined the Shaarey Zedek synagogue, and I was involved with the Betar movement of Zev Jabotinsky.

My children grew older and soon found their own life partners. Debra began dating Michael Feldman as a teenager. I remember the first time I met him after coming home from the grocery store. I teased him that, if he wanted to become my son-in-law, he would have to help me bring some bags in. He quickly responded, "Of course, Mrs. Perlstein." He was a charmer, and I could see that they were serious. When they got married, Debra was seventeen. They lived with us for three years, and soon I was a very young grandmother at forty-three years of age in 1967, when their beautiful daughter Lisa was born. They would go on to have three more children: Barry, Jay, and Eric.

My girlfriend Rosa Levinson helped set my daughter Rita up on a blind date with a very handsome Egyptian Jewish medical student named Joseph Salama. At first, Rita did not even want to go on the date, but I pleaded with her to go. After all, she didn't have to marry the guy! She finally relented and brought him into the house for me to meet him when they returned home that evening. I came down the stairs and almost fainted when I first laid eyes on my future son-in-law—he was *that* handsome. I had to lean on the piano to keep myself from falling over. They would soon get married and have three children: David, Evan, and Jill. Jill was the last of the grandchildren, and Harold would affectionately call her "my compote"—the sweet fruit dessert served at the end of a big meal.

My third daughter, Bonnie, went to school in Boston and also later met a wonderful man named Morry Levin. Morry worked at the nursing home, and Harold and I knew his parents. He had gone to law school. They would go on to have three daughters: Julie, and then the twins, Lauren and Dana.

At long last, I'd come to a place in my life where I could give full expression of my own desires. In particular, I longed to purchase a condo in Florida that I could mold to fit my style.

Chapter Fifteen

With my retirement and Harold slowing down, we decided to head to southern Florida and seek out a condo. Not able to find what we wanted immediately, we settled on purchasing a small condo for the time being, and also bought another one to invest in. When I spotted a larger condo to fit my dreams, we plunked down our rent money in a top-notch top area in Hallandale Beach overlooking the ocean. After a couple of years, I urged Harold to join me in buying it. I said, "Every year our rent goes up. It makes sense to buy and buy now." Purchased in 1980, this was to be my palace for thirty years.

The building housing the condo had a penthouse on the 20th floor. Two sides joined the common entrance and hallways. The higher up you lived, the bigger, better, and more expensive the condos were. Our condo was on the 12th floor on the right side. My heart and soul went into furnishing, designing, and decorating the interior. The value of the condo did increase year to year, and I only left it when I had to in 2012. The two smaller condos we had purchased were good rental investments. However, when a hurricane swept through the area and severely damaged them, we sold them off. Fortunately, we had enough insurance to cover the losses.

Harold went along with me on the condo, even though our marriage had begun to slip away. We were a great team, working together on the bars and nursing homes. But our monetary success had not been replicated in our homes or social life. While we were both committed to providing for our daughters well into the future, they had all grown up and married good men. It was time for me to come to terms with the fact that Harold and I simply weren't compatible.

Not fully recovered from the Holocaust, I had married Harold at an early, immature age out of fear of being left alone and penniless. I hadn't known who to turn to for help and support, I had lost my entire family and all my friends, and I really hadn't know what to do. We'd gotten married just a few days after reconnecting, and the age gap between us was substantial. While I'd tried to fit into Harold's lifestyle the best I could for the sake of our success and our children, from the start we'd been at odds with each other. We'd been together for almost thirty-four years, and, now that our daughters were grown and starting families of their own, I felt a need to move on to a new chapter in my life. I felt that nothing would ever change between us. Even though he urged me to drop the divorce proceedings, I did not reconsider.

The divorce proceedings continued to the finish. I was able to hold on to my beloved condo. My daughters remained close to me, and they rightly did not distance themselves from their father. I had no further ownership in the nursing home, which Harold had sold to our son-in-law (Debra's husband), Michael. I felt a burden had fallen from my shoulders. Harold did not wait long to re-marry, and, to me, the divorce was a breath of fresh air—a freedom I had not felt since childhood.

Picking up the pieces, I was welcomed into a group of active women in my age bracket. Among them were widows, divorcees, and singletons. They were lively and active. We enjoyed shopping together, checking new fashions, eating at great restaurants, seeing movies and theater performances, and winding up at the nearby dance hall. I formed some great friendships.

Most comforting in all those years was dwelling in my beautiful condo. I opened its doors to my friends and winter visitors, and it was a delight when my daughters and their families visited. Hallandale Beach was my home and favorite locality. I did still get to the Detroit area every year during Florida's humid summers.

I feel no regret or guilt over the divorce. Looking back, it turned out to be the right thing to do. Going at life alone helped me realize some of my most precious years.

Chapter Sixteen

While I had technically reached middle-age, my appearance belied my years. I felt active enough to dance, listen to music, go out with my friends, and keep up with current events. But I still had no thoughts about getting into a relationship with any man, though there were plenty of propositions and advances. My life was full, and I was freer than I'd ever been before. I thought I had it all.

But then came Ben.

I was sitting on a bench along the dance floor with my friends one night, chattering away and waiting for the music to start. A fine-looking man approached our bench, speaking to someone he knew who was sharing the bench with us.

"Let's squeeze together so he can sit down," I told my friends, and we all moved down so he had some room.

He sat next to me, we introduced ourselves to each other, and my world opened up. His name was Beno Sonders (short for Sonenschein), and he was a Polish Jew who had graduated as an engineer from a famed Krakow university, Jagalonean University. He was a fellow Holocaust survivor, having been imprisoned in the notorious Plaszow concentration camp. He had friends who were Schindler Jews, but he survived the camp, in part, due to his electrical engineering background. He was older than me, closer to Harold's age, but carried himself well. He dressed nicely, usually with a jacket and tie, but, above all, he was blessed with a gracious personality.

A widower, he'd lost both his wife and daughter at early ages, and his only close relative was a sister who was not much involved with him. He had long since retired from his electronics store in New York.

We enjoyed some small talk and danced together that night. Before the evening was over, we exchanged our phone numbers and addresses. Ben did not wait long to look me up. The next day, he came over to the condo complex and asked for me at the entrance desk. As he describes it, he blurted out, "Her first name is Bea—but I have forgotten her last name," and then he described me. Ben tried his best, and the security guard knew exactly who he was talking about when he said, "She is a very nice-looking woman with a great head of golden blonde hair."

"That's Mrs. Perlstein," the security guard said right away, helping him find my condo.

He proposed marriage in 1983, and I accepted. I spent eighteen very happy years married to Ben. Within our time together, he integrated himself with everybody, especially my daughters and family. The grandchildren affectionately called him Grandpa Ben, and he relished spending time with all of them. He fit in easily, and we never had an argument.

Death, however, cut all things short. First, it was Harold, who died in 1996 shortly after suffering a major stroke at our granddaughter's wedding at Shaarey Zedek in Southfield. Harold was well-known in the Detroit area, so the turnout at the funeral was huge.

Ben followed him in death a few years later in 2001, after suffering from a debilitating illness. His passing devastated me. I had spent eighteen glorious years with him, welcoming him into my home, the condo, and my heart. We'd traveled together and laughed together. All of that ended with his death, and it left me in a state of panic. I was completely alone.

My daughters realized my condition, and my daughter Bonnie and her husband Morry acted quickly to bring me closer to them. They dismantled everything in the condo, selling things off and finally selling the condo itself. I had no choice but to accept their wishes, and Bonnie found me an apartment near them with senior Jewish life accommodations.

My real joy in life, however, is to be near my daughters, grandchildren, and great-grandchildren. They are my greatest possessions and being able to see how my family has grown is truly unbelievable. I've watched them grow up before my very eyes and have always tried to counsel them as best I could. Even my frequent lectures about finding a Jewish mate had the best intentions. They often resulted in my daughters giving me a smile as they walked their boyfriends into the house and said, "Don't worry, Mom. He's Jewish."

I have so many fond memories of family that they would fill many more pages, but this is what I will leave you with. I cannot believe everything I went through and know that it is a miracle I survived. I went through the worst hell and nightmare imaginable, and hope and pray that no one in my family ever experiences what I endured. No matter how much anyone talks about it or how much people hear about it, it's not enough. You cannot begin to imagine what they did. People can scarcely believe that a civilized nation like Germany could do what they did.

To future generations, I say this: Let us be united as a people. We must pray for our country, and hope that Israel remains forever and ever. We need a place of refuge, our voice in the world. Beyond the Jewish community, the whole world needs to get along. The world needs to know what happened to us so that something like this never happens again.

While I have lived by many different names—Basia Gadziuk, Anna Kopera, and Basia Perlstein—I have no wish to be anyone but who I am today. I am proud of what I came from, and hold every struggle, hardship, and regret alongside my joys, happiness, and hope. I carry the voices and experiences of those who came before me—my mother, father, brother, and other family members and friends from David-Horodok. Through me and my descendants, I truly hope these memories will live on well into the future.

My name is Beatrice Sonders, and I am the last living Holocaust survivor of the Detroit David-Horodok Society.

Photographs

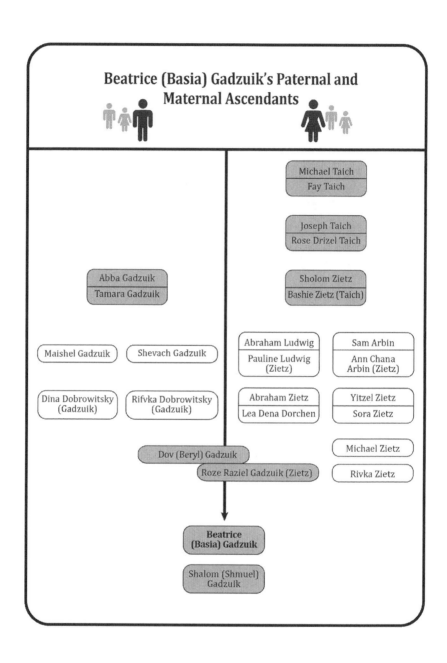

Beatrice (Basia) Gadzuik's Paternal and Maternal Ascendants

Michael Taich
Fay Taich

Joseph Taich
Rose Drizel Taich

Abba Gadzuik
Tamara Gadzuik

Sholom Zietz
Bashie Zietz (Taich)

Maishel Gadzuik

Shevach Gadzuik

Abraham Ludwig
Pauline Ludwig (Zietz)

Sam Arbin
Ann Chana Arbin (Zietz)

Dina Dobrowitsky (Gadzuik)

Rifvka Dobrowitsky (Gadzuik)

Abraham Zietz
Lea Dena Dorchen

Yitzel Zietz
Sora Zietz

Dov (Beryl) Gadzuik
Roze Raziel Gadzuik (Zietz)

Michael Zietz

Rivka Zietz

Beatrice (Basia) Gadzuik

Shalom (Shmuel) Gadzuik

92

The only known picture of Beryl
(Dov) Gadziuk, Basia's father. It
was mailed to his sister, Rifka, who
lived in Detroit.

The only known picture of Reizel
Gadziuk (Zietz), Basia's mother.
This was her passport photo, found
in a Nazi officer's desk after the
war. In 1961, Bea received it during
a visit to Israel.

The only picture of Basia and her brother Shalom, approximate ages 13 and 11. It was mailed to relatives in Detroit circa 1937.

גן־הילדים — 1929

שורה עליונה — מימין לשמאל: אברשה אולשנסקי, יהודית קצמן, ראובן מישלוב
שורה שנייה: שלישי מימין — שמעון מורץ; שני מימין — שישי מימין; שלישי משמאל — יהודה גיטלמן
שורה רביעית: שלישי משמאל — יעקב פריימן

A picture from a book printed in Israel in 1992, titled *The Tarbut School of David-Horodok*. The picture caption states it is the 1929 Kindergarten class. Beatrice identified herself as being the first girl on the right, standing in the second row. She also identified the principal, Mr. Oleshansky (standing far right), and her teacher, Berta (standing second from the left in the back row).

תלמידי בית־הספר מח"מכינה" וגן־הילדים, שדיברו אך ורק עברית וכונו "גורי בני יהודה" — 1934

Also from *The Tarbut School of David-Horodok*, this is a 1934 picture of "Ach V'Rak Ivrit" – a group of students who committed to speaking Hebrew at all times. It is believed Beatrice may be the sixth girl seated from the right in the second row, with her arms crossed.

95

The earliest known photo of Harold Perlstein, taken with his first wife Miriam in Sarny. Miriam and their daughter were killed during the liquidation of the Sarny ghetto.

Basia at the D.P. Camp Bad Reichenhall, in an outfit she sewed together out of a U.S. Army Green Blanket.

Basia and her friend Liza Wolf, in matching coats they made together. Wolf immigrated to Israel.

Basia's D.P. identification card.

Harold and Basia at a small park just outside the D.P. Camp Bad Reichenhall. This photo was taken by a friend who always looked for photographic subjects in the D.P. camp, whose last name was Narodovsky. Narodovsky later immigrated to Australia.

A photo of Harold and Basia prior to an evening out at the D.P. Camp Bad Reichenhall.

A photo of Harold and Basia prior to an evening out at the D.P. Camp Bad Reichenhall.

Beatrice holding her eldest daughter
Debra, age two and a half

Beatrice holding her second daughter
Rita in 1951, with Debra, age 5 (seated
to her right).

Bea with her Aunt Chana
Abrin. Her daughter Rita
is sitting on Harold's lap.

Beatrice and Harold in America, at the Bar Mitzvah of Robert Ludwig.

Beatrice and Harold in America.

Beatrice and Harold and Bea's aunt, Taunta Chana Abrin.

Mother's Day 1957. Beatrice bought matching outfits for her and her three daughters –
Debra, 12, Rita, 6, Bonnie, 3.

Portrait photo of Beatrice, circa 1958.

The Perlstein family at a
wedding, circa 1956, with
Rita (6) and Debra (10).

The Perlstein family at a wedding, circa 1959, with Bonnie (5), Rita (9), and Debra (13).

At the wedding of Beatrice's eldest daughter Debra in 1964. Left to right is Rita, Harold, Debra, Beatrice, and Bonnie.

Photo of Beatrice and her soon-to-be
son-in-law, Joseph Salama.

At the wedding of Beatrice's middle
daughter, Rita, in 1974.

Bea and Harold at the wedding of their youngest daughter Bonnie to Morry Levin.
Also pictured are Rita and Debra.

Beatrice with Beno Sonders at her condo in Hallandale, Florida.

Wedding of Beatrice and
Beno Sonders, with Beatrice's
three daughters, Rita, Bonnie,
and Debra.

Beatrice with cousin Dina Ashmann, the daughter of Harold's sister
Chaika Berko (Perlstein).

Beatrice with her cousin, Arnold Frumin, whose father, Victor, helped save Beatrice
by hiding her during the Sarny ghetto liquidation.

Beatrice Sonders reunited with her first cousin Ida Rosenblum (Dobrowitsky) in April of 2018 after research conducted using The Detroit Jewish News archive. Ida's mother, Rifka Dobrowitsky (Gadziuk), was the older sister to Bea's father, Beryl.

Photo provided by Ida Dobrowitsky from the wedding of her brother, Max. (From left to right) Ida, her father Morris, her mother Rifka, her brother Max, and the oldest sibling, Teibel.

Beatrice with all ten of her grandchildren: Dana, Lauren, and Julie Levin (left); Evan, Jill, and David Salama (center); Eric, Lisa, Barry, and Jay Feldman (right).

Beatrice with her three adult daughters: (from left to right) Rita Salama, Debra Feldman, and Bonnie Levin.

3 Generations
30 Direct line descendants

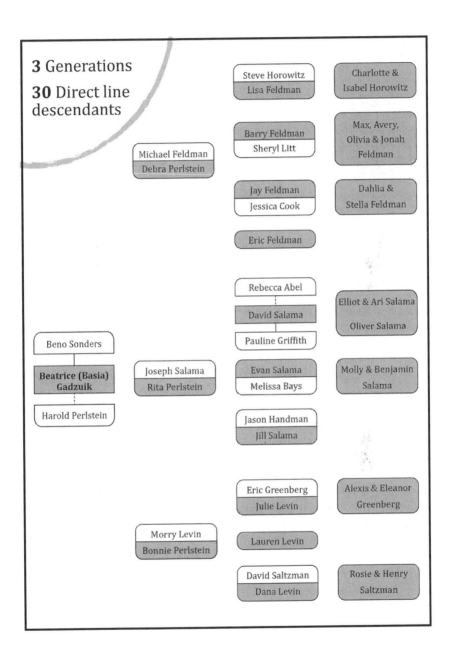

Steve Horowitz
Lisa Feldman

Charlotte & Isabel Horowitz

Michael Feldman
Debra Perlstein

Barry Feldman
Sheryl Litt

Max, Avery, Olivia & Jonah Feldman

Jay Feldman
Jessica Cook

Dahlia & Stella Feldman

Eric Feldman

Rebecca Abel

David Salama

Pauline Griffith

Elliot & Ari Salama

Oliver Salama

Beno Sonders

Beatrice (Basia) Gadzuik

Harold Perlstein

Joseph Salama
Rita Perlstein

Evan Salama
Melissa Bays

Molly & Benjamin Salama

Jason Handman
Jill Salama

Eric Greenberg
Julie Levin

Alexis & Eleanor Greenberg

Morry Levin
Bonnie Perlstein

Lauren Levin

David Saltzman
Dana Levin

Rosie & Henry Saltzman

Four generations (1997): Beatrice with oldest daughter Debra, first grandchild Lisa Feldman, and first great-grandchild Charlotte Horowitz.

Beatrice with her triplet set of great-grandchildren (2002): Avery, Olivia, and Jonah Feldman.

Beatrice with some of her great grandchildren (2016): Ari Salama, Charlotte Horowitz holding Dahlia Feldman, Elliot Salama holding Benjamin Salama, Isabel Horowitz holding Rosie Saltzman, Alexis Greenberg, and Molly Salama.

Beatrice with more of her great grandchildren at the Bat Mitzvah of Charlotte Horowitz (2008): Charlotte and Isabel Horowitz, Max, Avery, Jonah and Olivia Feldman, and Elliot Salama.

Beatrice with Elliot, Ari, and Oliver Salama during Passover, 2018.

Entrance to David-Horodok, with the city
name inscribed in Russian.

Original cobblestone-lined street in
David-Horodok.

View of the Horin River from the bridge that crosses it,
leading in and out of town.

One of the few remaining original homes from David-Horodok, dating back to the time of Basia, with a plaque memorializing the Jewish community of the town.

View looking back into town from the field that was once the Jewish cemetery, down the street from where Basia grew up.

The memorial at the mass grave of David-Horodok, seven kilometers outside the town.

A close-up of the English inscription at the mass grave outside David-Horodok. The inscription is also written in Yiddish, Polish, Hebrew, and Russian.

One of three mass graves located in a small forest on the outskirts of Sarny. The Hebrew on the plaque reads, "In memory of the Jews of Sarny, Rokitna, Dubrovytsya and the surrounding area that were murdered at the hands of the German Nazis and their helpers (may their names be obliterated) on the 13th and 14th day of the Hebrew month of Elul corresponding to August 26-27, 1942."

Second of three adjacent mass graves in a forest on the outskirts of Sarny, with the same marker as the first one.

Plaque on building in Sarny, commemorating the liquidation of the Sarny ghetto in 1942.

This soccer field, adjacent to the forest in which the mass graves are located in Sarny, was the Jewish cemetery of Sarny. The Germans, along with the local Ukrainians, destroyed the headstones of the cemetery during the war.

The Sluch River, north of Sarny, which Harold followed when he managed to escape from the ghetto liquidation in August of 1942.

Beatrice dancing the Hora at one of her grandchildren's weddings, 2003.

Made in the
USA
Columbia, SC